FLIGHT GUIDE FOR SUCCESS

Tips and Tactics for the Aspiring Airline Pilot

by
Captain Karen M. Kahn

Cheltenham Publishing

Cheltenham Publishing
933 Cheltenham Road
Santa Barbara, California 93105
www.AviationCareerCounseling.com
805 687 9493

Cover design by L.C. Crane
Text design by Carol Salvin

ISBN 0-9741723-0-8
Printed in the United States of America

Fly Smart —
Fly Safe!

Capt Kevin Koch

About the Author

Captain Karen M. Kahn has been actively involved in aviation for more than 35 years. She holds all ratings through ATP and was the first woman to be type-rated on the Lockheed JetStar. Her other ratings include flight engineer, seaplane, glider, helicopter, helicopter instrument, and Master Certificated Flight Instructor (MCFI) for instruments, multiengine, and airplanes.

Prior to starting her airline career in 1977, she instructed at Sierra Academy of Aeronautics (Oakland, CA) and later ran her own accelerated weekend ground school. At the present time, she's a captain for a major US air carrier and has flown the B727, DC-10, MD-80, and B757/767 on both domestic and international routes.

She's a frequent speaker at pilot seminars and career workshops. She has also written for various aviation publications, including AIR Inc.'s *Air Line Pilot Careers* magazine, AOPA's *Flight Training* magazine, *Flying Careers* magazine, *Woman Pilot*, and *International Women Pilots/99s News* magazines.

Karen specializes in helping pilots improve their flying and communication skills. She founded Aviation Career Counseling in 1989 to help pilots save time and money in their quest for a professional pilot's career. ACC offers personalized counseling for pilots of all experience levels, from people with zero flying time to retiring airline captains who want to continue flying professionally after their mandated retirement age.

Captain Kahn provides informative, insightful programs that show you how to fulfill your career dreams by using your own accomplishments to creatively market your unique skills and talents. You can contact her directly at www.AviationCareerCounseling.com for more details on available programs, including ACC's pilot career counseling and interview preparation services.

Acknowledgments

Many of the articles here have been revised and updated from their original appearance in various aviation magazines, including *International Women Pilots/99 News, Flying Careers, Woman Pilot, Air Line Pilot Careers,* and *AOPA Flight Training.* My special thanks go to Air, Inc. for their permission to adapt several articles that first appeared in *Air Line Pilot Careers* magazine.

As no book is ever written in a vacuum, I thank the many people who helped me put the 3rd edition of *Flight Guide* together. I appreciate all the input I've received—from casual readers who sent me their thoughts to my more critical aviation writer friends whose opinions I value highly.

Special thanks go to my husband, Captain John Clark, for his patience, encouragement, and endurance through some long sieges of indecision (to write or not to write a third edition) and frustration on my part.

My editor, Gayla Visalli, provided an enormous amount of constructive criticism during hours of challenging discussions, as well as a writer's refresher course to keep me from butchering the English language. I've learned how easily one's words can be misunderstood, by novices and professionals alike. After long years of experience in the cockpit where communications can often be difficult to hear, let alone understand, it is amazing to find out that misunderstanding can still occur when none of these external influences are present and one is merely reading the information on the printed page. Thank you, Gayla, for your patience when it came to saying it the way it had to be said in order that my meaning could be clearly understood by all readers. My patient book designer, Carol Salvin, deserves my thanks for enduring my fits and jerks of writing, rewriting, and editorial changes. And I thank my printing liaison, Van Bagley, for his helpfulness in educating me about the myriad ways a book can take shape.

Numerous pilots at Continental Airlines contributed their stories, which helped me explain the ins and outs of airline flying. Of particular value are how they accumulated the required flight time and the job progression they used to get to their goal of major airline pilot. Thank you one and all.

My thanks go to several patient airline captains who used their amateur photographic skills to help shoot the cover photo inside the Boeing 757 cockpit enroute from Houston to Los Angeles while commuting home from another series of my airline trips. And Larry Crane deserves special credit for incorporating the photo into a unique and captivating cover design.

I very much appreciate Rod Machado, Captain David Gwinn (TWA, ret.), Master CFI Greg Brown, and Captain Jean Harper not only for their kind comments but also their encouragement. Their numerous writings are required reading and a must for any pilot's permanent library.

Finally, I want to thank my father, Stephen Kahn, for insisting that I take a summer school typing course, thus making my writing efforts neat and readable.

Table of Contents

Chapter VII: Interview Basics

Chapter VIII: Interview Secrets

Chapter IX: Airline Flying

Glossary

Foreword

For a person just starting out in aviation–and sometimes even for one who has been flying a long time–the intricacies of securing a career in this field can be intimidating and confusing. Pilots are very much like actors, in that their choice of vocation is passionately pursued by many, and great hardships and indignities are willingly endured, just to have a shot at a dream, in our case a career in the cockpit of something large and fast.

Anyone wishing to demystify the process, however, could save much time and wasted effort with the proper guidance. This book, written by an airline captain and aviation career counselor, covers a variety of subjects, ranging from the concrete mechanics of finding a flying job to the subtle nuances of attitude and personal presentation. The advice is based on time-tested experience and common sense, with a wide, nonprejudicial overview on many topics not normally touched on in such detail by other "how to" publications.

Aviation aspirants want honest, straight talk; that is what they will get from *Flight Guide for Success* by Captain Karen M. Kahn. With a background that spans the spectrum from small general aviation airplanes to the latest in high-tech jet transports, Captain Kahn offers valuable direction based on the best of her own experiences as well as those of hundreds of other successful pilots. The articles are tightly written, with an emphasis on the facts, honest encouragement, and effectiveness. Hints and suggestions are included that can save readers much time and frustration and ultimately help present themselves in the most professional manner possible.

As an airline captain who took the "hard road," with little in the way of useful guidance when I was first starting out, I've always had an interest in helping others avoid the same trial-and-error process I endured. Captain Kahn's timely and helpful advice is a valuable step toward reaching this most worthwhile career goal.

Jean E. Harper
Captain, United Airlines

Introduction

The continual sharing of information among aviators has to be one of aviation's greatest assets—as well as an enormous safety feature. How many times have you heard a flying story that sent chills down your spine and made you wonder how you would have reacted if you had experienced that same event? Then months or years later, when a similar situation arose, you recalled that story and thought twice about your proposed action, which possibly changed the outcome or broke a deadly chain of events.

Because we all benefit greatly from aviation's educational aspect, I've enjoyed sharing my experience and knowledge through feature articles in aviation magazines and have adapted many of these pieces for this book. A number of them were written in response to questions frequently asked by pilots during career counseling sessions my partner and I have conducted at our company, Aviation Career Counseling. Others arose out of mistakes or misunderstandings common to pilots everywhere. Some articles highlight omissions to common knowledge that could benefit all of us if only someone would take the time to write about them.

This book is meant to be read in any order that benefits the reader. For novices this may mean starting at the beginning and reading all the sections sequentially. Advanced pilots might want to skip directly to a particular area of concern—resume writing or interviewing, for example.

Communication is a key to learning. In almost every article you'll find that the ability to express yourself is the common thread that binds events together. If you enjoy this book, 1 hope you'll pass it along to any friends who might benefit from knowing more about flying—our passion!

Captain Karen M. Kahn
October 1997

Update, September 2003

Aviation will always will be a major fascination to many people. After the events of 9/11/2001, 1 thought about reprinting and updating *Flight Guide* and was curious to know if the effects of that traumatic event had changed the enthusiasm of people who are, to put it simply, airplane crazy. Fortunately, as the world returned to a somewhat normal state, 1 found that the same passions still exist and may actually have been heightened by the tragedies of 9/11.

For you who enjoy just one more purposeful hangar tale, welcome aboard. For those of you who are new to aviation, you're about to enter an exciting and challenging world.

Stay focused, fly safely, keep your eyes open for other pilots who are passionate about flying, and spread our aviation gospel.

Captain Karen M. Kahn
Santa Barbara, CA
www.AviationCareerCounseling.com

CHAPTER 1

GETTING STARTED

Planning Your Aviation Career

How do I plan a career as a pilot? What's involved in the training and how long will it take? What kinds of jobs are available and what can I expect thereafter? What if I'm not interested in flying for an airline? Are there other types of good-paying jobs? How do I decide what's best for me? You should ask yourself these kinds of questions before venturing into any new field, but they are especially important for pilots.

Flying differs from other career endeavors in that many pilots start flying as a hobby, sport, or recreational pastime, and this casual involvement leads to a real passion for flying, which then makes them wonder how they can do for a living what they like to do anyway. In my mind, feeling the thrill and excitement of flying is a very necessary ingredient for an airline career. Now, let's assume that you've got the desire and are wondering how to turn that desire into your life's work. Understand that you still have to face a long, hard road of training and accumulating hours of experience to reach the top. But that passion will help you enjoy, not just endure, the whole career path and, like an addict, keep you coming back for more.

Planning your career will take some careful consideration as well as a lot of investigation and inquiry into the alternatives available. You should learn about the requirements that make up each license or certificate you need to acquire

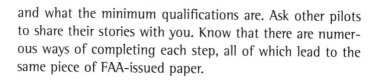

and what the minimum qualifications are. Ask other pilots to share their stories with you. Know that there are numerous ways of completing each step, all of which lead to the same piece of FAA-issued paper.

A Basic Plan

Your basic plan should begin with obtaining your Private Pilot Certificate—40 to 70 hours of training, roughly half as dual instruction and half as solo practice—which, like most licenses, requires a written test as well as an oral and practical examination at its conclusion. If you are prone to "checkitis"—that dreaded fear of taking checkrides—you may want to rethink your career aspirations because this one aspect will always be with you and become even more pronounced as you progress.

After finishing your Private, you'll need to gain experience and self-confidence by flying to new places, both with and without passengers, during the day as well as at night. After you accumulate about 100 hours, your next step is to learn about instrument flying, or flying solely by reference to the aircraft's instruments. It's a new world of procedures and precision maneuvers that is probably the most important rating you'll ever receive. Throughout your pilot career, your instrument flying skills will be tested and retested, so make sure you devote the proper time and attention to this fundamental area.

Upon completing your Instrument Rating, you should obtain your Commercial Pilot Certificate, which will allow you to fly for hire or, said another way, make it legal for you to receive compensation for your flying labor. Soon afterward, or even possibly before, you should consider adding a Multiengine Rating to your license so you can start logging hours in a twin-engine aircraft; this is the type of time that most pilot employers require and value most highly.

Flight Instructor Ratings (Basic, Instrument, and Multiengine) will not only provide what may be your first flying income but also teach you the finer points of flying and help you acclimatize to flying from the right seat. If you aspire to a flying career in a multipilot cockpit, this experience will provide you with many important benefits, not the least of which is showing that you're serious about becoming a professional pilot.

To reach this point in your journey toward a pilot career, you'll likely spend between $15,000 and $25,000 and possibly more. Your flight time will be in the 350- to 400-hour range, and your work will just have begun. But remember, it's enjoyable work that will contribute greatly to your skills and hireability as a pilot. Most jobs for low-time pilots, those with less than 1,000 hours, are local ones obtained by networking with flight schools and airplane owners while completing your training. Sharing your love of flying with others can often net you more opportunities than other job-search techniques.

> Most jobs for low-time pilots, those with less than 1,000 hours, are local ones obtained by networking with flight schools and airplane owners while completing your training.

Pilots like to help pilots who help themselves and who are willing to work hard for their rewards. Your job is to demonstrate to those who can help you that you're ready, willing, and able to pay your dues and will put any opportunity they give you to good use. Demonstrating that you are a thorough, conscientious, and safe pilot will provide others with the evidence they need to trust you with their lives and livelihoods.

A job offer despite low flying time is often obtained through being in the right place at the right time. (We need someone to fly right seat of our light twin; are you, my instructor who has taught me faithfully, available?) Or it might come from starting a business, as I did, that allows you to fly an aircraft from place to place. Taking the initia-

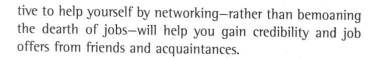

tive to help yourself by networking—rather than bemoaning the dearth of jobs—will help you gain credibility and job offers from friends and acquaintances.

Complete your ratings as quickly as possible.

You should plan your strategy so you can complete each step on the pilot's ladder at the earliest opportunity. Finishing all your ratings in minimum time can pay big benefits later, when you discuss your training history with a potential employer. Hiring "go-getters" is much easier than hiring "ho-hummers," and airlines look closely at efforts you made to accelerate your own progress. Are you focused and dedicated? What sacrifices have you made for your flying career? With good answers to these questions, you'll substantially increase your chances of being hired by both corporate and airline employers.

However, don't feel you have to nail down all of your career considerations at one time as you begin your love affair with airplanes and flying. Ask lots of questions, sample numerous answers, and enjoy the fun, excitement, and freedom that comes from learning a new skill. Aviation has provided a lifetime of satisfaction and enjoyment for many people just like you.

Is an Aviation Career Right for Me?

Let's assume you have a Private License and about 200 hours of flight time and that you *love* flying with a passion. You've been looking for something that excites you and now you're wondering if you should get into aviation full-time? Well, let's see if you've got the strong underlying motivation to weather the ups and downs of the industry.

First of all, just how much do you really love flying? Are you the kind of person who looks for an excuse to hang out at the airport? Or do you just head out there during your free time to watch airplanes and talk flying with other pilots? Does a job at the airport, including line service, reception, dispatching, or washing airplanes, appeal to you? Would you like to spend most of your free time at the airport or would that get boring after a while?

> If you're really hooked on flying, you'll find yourself devouring everything you can about airplanes.

If you're really hooked on flying, you'll find yourself devouring everything you can about airplanes. Flying will occupy most, if not all, of your free time and drive you to spend most of your waking hours thinking and scheming about how to do more flying. On the other hand, if it's just a fun avocation, something you enjoy doing every now and then, you'll probably do better spending your energies elsewhere. Aviation requires a lot of passion, perseverance, and dedication. There's a built-in qualifier to weed the wannabes from the truly dedicated ones. It's a long, difficult, and expensive journey to acquire the credentials needed to get a job—and the apprenticeship is probably the worst of any profession around. That's the bad news. The good news you already know—you'll be able to hang around airplanes to your heart's content.

The big question is can you afford to do it? For some of you, the question is, can you afford *not* to? If the poor pay, long hours, and years of playing second fiddle to more experienced aviators doesn't bother you, then think seriously about getting some good advice on how to go about realizing your dream.

Do I Need A College Degree?

How much education is required for a job as a pilot with an airline? Let's start with the most restrictive—a major U.S. airline. Virtually everyone hired has a minimum of a four-year degree and many have a master's degree or a total of six or more years of college. Airlines may not state an education requirement, but they will hire *first* those with the best credentials.

Does that mean your chances are nil with 2 years or less of college? Not necessarily. If you are a member of a minority group (female or noncaucausian male), you will be competing mostly with others in your situation. If you are white and male, the competition will be much stiffer. Regardless of your status, having more education is definitely better, but is always part of a package. That is, how do you measure up when all of your qualifications are considered together?

Ways to improve your hireability

One way you can improve your hireability is by adding various extras to your application that help a prospective employer realize you're aware of your deficiencies and are working on them. Enroll at a local college and show your current status on your application. If you can't afford the time to take classes, look into some of the alternative schools that give credit for life experience and offer a variety of training options (on-line, correspondence, part-time attendance) to help you complete your degree. These days, much of your own experience, including flight ratings and special aviation training courses you've already completed, can easily be turned into college credits from an accredited institution.

Perhaps you're working for a company that has a learn-while-you-earn program that will help you finance the cost of your higher education. Another possibility is to combine flight training with a learn-while-you-earn program at a school that gives college credit for flight ratings and employs its students as well. These are combinations to consider before discounting yourself as being short on education and hence not hireable.

Smaller airlines are usually more lenient on the education rule. When pilot hiring at major airlines picks up, the other airlines find their supply of applicants is limited. Minimum qualifications (including flight times, ratings, education, and experience) will be adjusted according to what is available among the applicants. Remember, however, that education is a mirror of how well you'll do in that airline's training program. If you have very little education and come across as lacking in vocabulary, life skills, and street smarts, you'll find employers using the "not enough education" excuse to move on to an applicant who will represent them better to the travelling public.

Even if you're short on formal schooling, never presume that you're unqualified for a job. Instead, assume that you're unique and have a range of special qualities that distinguish you from other applicants. Highlight your talents and accomplishments. Some interviewers may be more impressed by your personality and presentation than by a string of degrees from some institute of higher learning. Sometimes an explanation as to why you didn't finish/start your degree, as well as why your grades were perhaps less than sterling, can help offset what might be considered a minus on your application. It's your job to sell yourself. If you don't sing your own praises, who will?

Big School or Small School?

One of the few universal decisions faced by pilots at some time during their careers has to do with what kind of training to choose. Does the large flight school or training facility really have the edge over a small one? Does it actually matter where you train?

Arguments can be made for both options. Big schools frequently have much broader educational opportunities, an important plus if you plan to acquire an academic degree while completing your flight training. Small schools, on the other hand, often expose students to more types of flying and future job possibilities because they deal with both based and transient aircraft in addition to their own training fleet. You will also save money on living and transportation expenses if the school is local. If you seek the structured learning of a large school but can only afford to attend a small local one, talk with your instructors about the possibility of duplicating some of the big-school type of training and scheduling to help you accelerate your progress.

As you investigate your local airport's offerings and those within an hour's driving time, you will also learn a lot about the going rates for aircraft rentals and instructors in your area and quickly become familiar with the requirements for your particular rating or certificate.

Surveying the field

There are numerous good articles on how to choose a flight school, and I recommend you read up on the subject before you interview your candidates. Arm yourself with a list of questions to ask your prospects and write down your observations as well as comments from current students you encounter during your visit. Don't forget a visit to their maintenance shop as well as a chat with other businesses on the field to see if they have any comments that might be pertinent to your inquiry.

The usual questions of how much it costs and how long it will take are, of course, important. But, you should also interview past students to learn their thoughts about the training they received, probing for both positive and negative comments. Ask them if they had the chance to do it over again, would they change anything? For the price of a long distance phone call you could easily discover an important detail (like they *never* hire their graduates, or their twin course *won't* qualify you to rent any of their multiengine airplanes) which may have been conveniently omitted in their web, printed, or on-site sales presentation.

For a professional pilot course, you'll see ads ranging from $14,000 to $40,000 and up. The reasons for price variations can range from school size (larger ones often tend to be more expensive), and types of aircraft flown (do I need to start off in a larger 4-place airplane?) to hours of dual versus solo flight, instructor rates, and books, supplies, and checkride fees. Add to tuition the costs of transportation and lodging if the locale is a distant one.

Do airlines care about your choice of school?

In the overall scheme of things, what kind of a school you attend—large or small, big name or no-name—to get your basic ratings (Private, Instrument, Commercial, Multiengine) is of more interest to you than to your future employer. As a matter of fact, once you're past the training stage, boasting about your attendance at a school certified under a particular part of the Federal Aviation Regulations (Part 61 or Part 141) tends to label you as a lightweight who has overdosed on advertising hype. Provide the information if asked, but realize that it's not of particular interest to a future airline employer.

In the overall scheme of things, what kind of a school you attend—large or small, big name or no-name—to get your basic ratings is of more interest to you than to your future employer.

We're not discussing here special proprietary programs that require advance screening and attendance at a specific school. If you plan to participate in one of these programs, be sure you understand exactly what you're getting: very specialized training aimed at a specific job. Also, recognize that the same dollars expended over a similar time period could provide you with three to four times the flight hours and several additional ratings/licenses, had you chosen a normal pro pilot program. Make sure you actually need the education and training you're buying to achieve your personal goal, not just buying what a salesman on commission wants to sell you.

Although most major airlines aren't especially concerned with the details of your primary training, they are *very* interested in your overall education, total flight time, and kind of job you presently hold. Don't chose a big-name flight school thinking it will substantially improve your chances of getting hired unless you personally know that to be the case or the school can provide you with some type of guarantee— which is very rare. Recognize that attendance at a big school, by its nature, makes you a small fish in a big pond. Jobwise, you're competing for available opportunities with many more pilots than you would be at a smaller school.

Another advantage of training at a small school is that you may have a chance of landing a job with the school itself because the competition is greatly reduced and you'll have more opportunity to network with those who do the hiring. Should you wish to work in a particular location, remember that schools tend to hire the people they have trained, rather than those who walk in the door, even with a "big-school" degree. They know personally the pilot they'll be hiring, and you'll know the details of the work environment in which you'll be expected to perform.

Once you've done your homework, get some advice from an impartial source who understands your situation and has no financial stake in your decision. Remember that your success in finding future employment will be mostly a result of your own perseverance and networking efforts, rather than the size of the school you've attended.

Age: Not the Factor
It Once Was

When I began my airline career in 1977, age was a big stumbling block for airlines, many of which had a stated maximum hiring age of 30 (though I'm pleased to report that we had a new hire in my class who was 37—an old man by our under-30 standards. He had received special dispensation for having spent 7 years as a Vietnam POW). Now, more than 25 years later, the average hiring age for an airline pilot is close to 35. If you're interested in a midlife career change, you may be wondering whether you should jump into the fray. Let's take a look at some of the issues you'll want to explore to help you make that decision.

The original intent of an upper age limit was based on amortizing the expensive training for new hires over the maximum number of years. With an upper hiring age limit of 30, airlines had at least 30 years (until a pilot reached the mandatory retirement age of 60) to recoup their investment. Now, with age discrimination looming as a legal deterrent, airlines no longer list upper age limits, preferring to consider pilot qualifications on their own merits. The age barriers, per se, are seemingly gone, leaving only the requirement that you meet their other pilot qualifications.

Advantages of maturity

If you're in your 30s, it's certainly not impossible to become an airline pilot, as long as you're willing to devote the time, patience, and money required. Recognize that as an older pilot you'll have the advantages that maturity brings and, very likely, another marketable skill to fall back on when times get tough and pilot lay-offs occur. You'll also have numerous contacts from various walks of life to help accelerate your training plan. Network with friends, family, and other pilots, particularly those who own airplanes, to determine if they might be good sources for time building, plane sharing, or job referrals to move you toward your goal.

Hopefully, you've got some savings and a good credit rating to help you forge ahead, whereas a young pilot often lacks these essentials. Think about making your transition to full-time flying slowly, so you can keep your income source intact until the day you find you can survive on a full-time pilot's salary, which may be a fraction of what you're making at your present job.

Don't set impossible goals for yourself. You didn't achieve your current workplace status overnight, so don't expect to transition to aviation with minimal effort. Your future employer will appreciate your careful, considered transition and recognize that you're serious about your career change if you show that you've made well-timed steps that reflect realistic planning. When you're being questioned at your first airline interview as to why you chose to switch careers in midstream, you can show them the sacrifices you've made and your dedication to a pilot career.

Remember, too, if you act, fly, and talk on the radio like a mature professional, you'll likely gain the respect due someone with more total flying time. And who's to tell them any different? There's no reason to reveal the fact that you've got only 200 hours when you act and fly like a 900-hour pilot. That's not to say you should deceive someone about your credentials. Instead, impress them with your maturity, good sense, attention to detail, and concern for providing a high-quality service. An excellent performance will make them want to hire you, regardless of your resume statistics.

An additional bonus if you're an older pilot who has some prior flight time—say, a Private or Commercial Pilot certificate and several hundred hours over the past 5 to 10 years—is that if someone asks you when you started flying, you can mention the year, smile, and not mention your total time. Let them assume you're an experienced pilot rather than blurting out your logbook statistics. Once again, what's left unsaid can often be the key to unlocking an elusive job opportunity. Obviously, you'll not want to spend 10 years getting your flight time totals up to the magic 1,500 hours total time with 200 multi, but don't feel you have to finish up in 6 months, either.

Networking and bartering pay off.
The art of networking in aviation is a time-honored process. Strive to cultivate people who can help you with future employment, making repeated contacts, if necessary, to strengthen the networking bond.

If you are a seasoned employee in any field, you might devise a plan to use your current skills as exchange media for flying time. Who knows, your ability as a hot-shot programmer may be just what a local aircraft owner needs in his business, and you may find a win/win situation trading your skills for flight time. Accountants, lawyers, real estate agents, dentists, and chiropractors (just to name a few I've flown with) have succeeded in using their basic skills as trade media while training for advanced ratings. Bartering allows them to keep the costs down as they pay their dues in the aviation world.

Being too old is mostly a state of mind. It's up to you to scrutinize your available resources and determine what you're willing to sacrifice to realize your lifelong dream of becoming a professional pilot.

Midlife Career Change: Is Faster Better?

As a pilot career counselor, I am seeing more mature beginning pilots who want to fulfill their life's dream and become a professional pilot. Many have harbored the dream since childhood, while others have read just enough to wonder if this might be the passion they've been looking for—and a way to escape a dreary nine-to-five desk-bound job.

One inevitable topic of discussion during our counseling sessions is the quickie "zero time to pro pilot in six months" option. Such a plan naturally appeals to those in their 30s and 40s who feel this route will allow them to make up for lost time and enter the job market sooner. Is there a distinct advantage to this shortcut or does following the longer, more traditional training scenario make for a better chance of succeeding in this plum profession? The second option is usually better. Although it's certainly possible to complete the necessary training in a short three- to six-month period, the result can often be likened to a beached whale. He knows how to swim, but getting close enough to the environment he's familiar with can be a bit tricky and require a great deal of assistance.

What we're really talking about is short-circuiting the experience requirements for pilots who fly larger multicrew airplanes. Just how does a new hire fare once on the line, having to perform in other than standard conditions, particularly if his or her total aviation experience is limited to a short three to six months of flying?

Let's start with the admission that once we've passed our youth, our ability to study and learn new skills becomes somewhat diminished, and what we could once have gulped down by the glassful now needs to be sampled and sipped as we reach midlife. In professional aviation, it's crucial that you match your training speed to your learning ability so you don't collect any pink slips along the way.

> In professional aviation, it's crucial that you match your training speed to your learning ability so you don't collect any pink slips along the way.

The Pilot Records Improvement Act allows employers to carefully scrutinize your records and a pattern of checkride failures, accidents, or incidents can mean death to that airline career you've been dreaming about—and paying for with your hard-earned life's savings, or worse, with a high-interest-rate loan.

Experience versus book learning

According to my flight operations management mole, experienced pilots—those who've learned through trial and error and by teaching the skills to others—make markedly better regional first officers. Those who've learned their lessons through "speed study" and rote memorization often have insufficient PIC hours to help them when it comes to making decisions and judging wisely the best solution to a particular problem. If I had to assess the value of my book learning versus the "been there, done that" system, I'd certainly pick the latter as offering much more substance and inspiring greater confidence.

Just recently, I told my new-hire first officer that he likely knew the "book work" on our airplane better than I did because he had just finished ground school, and it's been

15-plus years since I attended initial training. However, my 10,000-plus hours on the MD80 has shown me a lot—if I can remember it all! So let's work together to benefit from our respective resources. Using the same logic, I once declined a Part 91 solo flight in a friend's well-equipped F33 Bonanza because I knew that my lack of recent experience in the type, some questionable weather conditions, and the onset of night would make for a set-up I felt ill-equipped and unwilling to handle. My vast flying experience led me to conclude that the conditions were not right for me to make a comfortable, non-stressful flight.

While we're talking about experience, let's look at the fiscal benefits of gaining some longevity in this business. Because your initial training will put a strain on your savings, try to make the transition to full-time flying a gradual one so that you can keep your income from your old job while you ease into the aviation world. Remember, your first pilot job is going to pay you a very small part of what you've probably been earning. Keeping two incomes as long as possible makes good sense and is another key to making a successful midlife career change.

Adaptability and flexibility—two crucial attributes of a good pilot, particularly in the airline world—are much easier to acquire when one has the experience to back up the decision-making process. Trying to succeed in the constantly changing world of aviation is so much more difficult when your frame of reference is very narrow. A year or two of seeing how it's really done can be invaluable and increase your chances for success. The ticking clock will definitely favor the pilot who's seen enough mistakes to anticipate his own and has learned the value of patience and foresight when it comes to carving out a niche in an airliner's cockpit.

CHAPTER 2

SKILLS AND STRATEGIES

The Networking Factor

One of the best kept secrets in aviation is what I call the networking factor. Simply stated, everyone who's been successful in aviation has been helped by someone, somewhere along the way. It's an unwritten rule that each of us who benefits from this system is obligated to return the favor and make the "payback" in the form of helping some other deserving pilot. The key word here is "deserving." Helping someone who's going to appreciate the assistance and put your efforts to good use is almost as important as the help itself. You'd hate to assist someone who wasn't serious and later find they'd wasted

> Show them you're hard-working, conscientious, dedicated, and passionate about your flying.

the effort you made on their behalf. The idea, then, is to "pay it forward" (like the film of the same name) and when you accomplish your goals, help someone else get a start—just as you received that leg up when you were struggling to make a go of it.

So, you'll have to spend a good part of your airport hours talking with as many other pilots as possible, taking an interest in what's going on, expressing your desire to learn all you can, and generally acting like the kind of person you'd like to help get ahead. Then you must prove your worth by demonstrating you'll put this special assistance to good use. How? By showing that you're the kind of pilot who will carry on the traditions we all admire and will make others proud to have helped you accelerate your career. Show them you're hard-working, conscientious, dedicated, and passionate about your flying.

The specifics of networking depend on your particular situation. You may have to do some serious research on the areas you want to target. If there's a specific company that interests you, become acquainted with key personnel there and learn as much as you can about their aviation needs. If there is a certain individual who might help you, direct your efforts toward that person by frequenting the same venues and informally introducing yourself to become acquainted. If informal contact isn't possible, a formal approach may be necessary, perhaps using what's called an informational interview.

The informational interview

The key to networking is to express your interest and desire in a person or firm without being obnoxious or patronizing. One approach is to seek an informational interview, in which your goal is to speak with an individual who can help you without actually asking him or her to do anything specific for you. You want to obtain suggestions as to how you can best navigate the aviation get-a-job maze in your journey to an airline career. What, for example, does he or she recommend you do to widen your circle of acquaintances? Is there anyone you should contact who might be of help to you? If this person were in your shoes, who would he or she contact and how often? Would taking a particular course or getting a certain type of flight time be helpful in your quest? Is there any specific reading you might do or are there other actions you could take to get ahead?

You are picking the brain of your subject and, at the same time, impressing him or her with your serious interest and determination. Hopefully, your actions will convince him to take a chance and hire you, should an opening become available. What you *don't* say, is "hire me." Instead, you solicit ideas and opinions and then put that information to work, demonstrating by your actions that you're worthy of the help you're *not* asking for. Once you've completed the interview, be sure to keep your contact informed of your progress, detailing what you've done with their suggestions. After your first meeting, send a short thank you note and then follow up, at least quarterly, with a note or greeting card containing a few lines describing your current status, progress, and short-term goals.

Keep a card file on your key contacts, listing for each one your initial meeting date, the person's aviation and business interests, telephone numbers, addresses, e-mail address, and the kind of contact you made. Saving articles or clippings of interest can provide a reason to recontact this person, eliminating that "won't he think me pushy to keep bothering him?" possibility. When you pass a new milestone—such as a new rating, more flight time, some award, or accomplishment—pass that on to your contacts in the form of a short note highlighting your successes.

More approaches

Attend as many local and national industry meetings and seminars as possible. Even if you're not personally fascinated by a local airport board meeting, it may be your next networking opportunity. One pilot I know got his start in commuter aviation by introducing himself to the Director of Operations for a new airline who came to the local airport commission meeting to describe his company's inaugural service to this pilot's hometown. Wanting to hire pilots who lived in the area, he was delighted to meet my friend and eventually hired him.

Always carry a supply of professional-looking business cards as well as your updated resume. The cards should be tasteful, not trendy, listing your name, ratings, and an address, phone number, and e-mail. Your resume, which you should keep in a folder in your car or briefcase, should be dated and include a self-addressed envelope and your business card. Being well-prepared will impress your subject—as will your professional appearance, appropriate, of course, to the event in question. Remember pilots have a public image to uphold. Make sure your first meeting with any prospective employer reflects favorably on your ability to handle public situations.

It has been said that what's important in networking is *who* you know. Equally, important, I feel, is who knows *you* and your capabilities. Now is not the time to be modest. Sing your own praises. If you don't, who will?

Which Rating, When?

A frequent question asked by aspiring professional pilots is "which ratings or certificates should I get and in what order?" For that matter, does the order of your training make any real difference?

Let's begin with a quick review of certificates versus ratings. A certificate is the type of pilot's license you hold: Student, Private, Commercial, CFI or ATP (we'll leave out Recreational for the time being). Ratings are appended to licenses once you've demonstrated your proficiency and passed the required tests, such as Instrument, Multiengine, Instrument Instructor, and Glider.

The normal progression, once you have completed your Private Certificate, is to start working on your Instrument Rating. This is an excellent way to build flight hours and experience until you reach the required total time for a Commercial Certificate. Your "gray sky card" is probably the most important rating you'll ever obtain, and it behooves you to pay close and serious attention to the learning involved in the art of flying blind inside the clouds.

The next goal for most pilots is normally the Commercial Certificate, which allows you to charge for piloting services. Until that point, you may share expenses with your passengers, but regulations forbid you to actually charge them. Once you've got the skill to be paid, you'll want to obtain your teaching credential (Certificated Flight Instructor or

CFI) to gain more experience and flight hours. The advanced flight instructor ratings (CFII for Instrument Flight Instructor) will broaden your knowledge and permit you to give (and charge more for) advanced instruction. Somewhere along the way, you should obtain a twin-engine or Multiengine Rating to add to your Commercial Certificate.

Too often, little thought is given to the how and when of obtaining a Multiengine Rating. You should start thinking about that rating early in your career, normally after you obtain your Commercial Certificate. Since most professional pilot jobs place a great deal of emphasis on total multiengine time logged, getting the ME Rating can be your ticket to quickly building valuable twin time. How and when you complete it can also be of importance to your career.

When should you get a Multiengine Rating?

If you see an opportunity to log some twin time, for instance, if you have friends who own a twin or there's one for rent at your flight school, then plan to take your training as soon as you finish your Instrument Rating. If you complete your ME Rating prior to acquiring the Instrument Rating, you'll be limited to VFR only and will have to repeat a portion of the flight check to demonstrate your instrument proficiency in a twin. But, if you have a good opportunity to log ME time while working on your Instrument Rating, then don't worry about the repeat check; by all means, complete your ME training as soon as possible.

Some flight schools will suggest that you wait to obtain your ME until after you complete the CFI ratings. I feel it's important to have the ability to log ME time early in your career. You never know when you'll encounter a situation where you can ride along on a charter and perhaps get some PIC (Pilot-in-Command) time on the deadhead (FAR Part 91 not-for-hire) leg back to home base. If you're rated, you can log the time. If not, you have to hope that the PIC is a CFI, and only then could you log the flight as dual received.

How to get the Multiengine Rating

There are usually two or three options in training programs for a Multiengine Rating. If you're learning at a flight school that has multiengine equipment available, I'd certainly get my rating there. Your total time in type will increase and put you that much closer to meeting the insurance requirements for PIC and hence able to rent the aircraft.

If you have a job opportunity to fly a specific type of twin, say a Cessna 310 or a Beech Baron, you may want to seek out a multiengine course that uses that type to become more familiar with it. You may have to pay more or go some distance to find an available airplane or instructor, but it will be worth it if it makes your entry into the job market an easier one.

Finally, there's the quickie, two- or three-day course that offers a Multiengine Rating in the minimum time, frequently in minimum equipment. This is a good solution for someone who needs the rating quickly and isn't concerned with logging time in a specific type or establishing a relationship with a school in order to meet time-in-type requirements.

However you train, be sure you get a good foundation in multiengine theory. Although there's no written exam required, the knowledge needed to fly a twin safely is important. Several good books are available as well as numerous audio and video tapes. For those of you who are presently ME pilots there's also a good cassette series called The *Pilots Audio Update*, which provides numerous segments on topics of interest to all pilots with specific emphasis on instrument and multiengine flying. Edited by Richard Taylor, the well-known aviation author, the series is available from Belvoir Publications at 800/424-7877.

For the professional pilot-to-be, the order of ratings *is* important. You can save yourself time and money by carefully considering how, when, and where to complete the requirements when planning your flight training.

Spending Your Flying Dollars Wisely

Flying dollars have been misspent by most pilots at one time or another. And foolish spending is not limited to novices. I've heard numerous tales of woe, from beginners and seasoned pros alike, about buying goods and services they thought would benefit their flying careers but didn't.

> Flying is a lifelong dream for many, and when the opportunity arises to fulfill that dream, people often toss normal caution and common sense to the wind.

As a pilot career counselor, one of my biggest jobs is to try to save budding pilots from their own ignorance and over-enthusiasm. Flying is a lifelong dream for many, and when the opportunity arises to fulfill that dream, people often toss normal caution and common sense to the wind. If it's flying, they want it now; and if it's expensive, that must make it better and therefore even more necessary for their successful entree into their dream world of flying.

The road to success in a pilot's career can be littered with many high-dollar potholes. They range from overspending on basic training to unnecessary expenditures for seemingly professional add-ons, such as "job-qualification" courses that familiarize students with a large airline-type aircraft. Such gimmicks sound inviting to the aspiring airline pilot who hopes that this bit of extra knowledge will make his resume shine.

"Big-Bucks Basic Training" Programs

Flight training is a business just like any other enterprise, and many newcomers forget that recruiters from flight schools are paid to do their jobs. You should keep in mind that all FAA licenses and ratings ultimately appear on the same wallet-sized card, regardless of where your training was obtained.

One pilot told me how impressed he was to have a certain school's recruiter come to his home to explain their flight programs to him and his family. I suspect this fellow is too young to remember the days of door-to-door encyclopedia salesmen, but the idea is just the same—it's their job! A year or so into the program, when all his initial classmates had dropped out, he found himself deeply in debt and was now faced with declaring bankruptcy. As we discussed his alternatives, he began to realize that perhaps he'd been too quick to swallow the recruiter's glib sales pitch. This was a truly sad story, fueled by insufficient knowledge and an understandable yearning to fly.

One of the unadvertised benefits of aviation is that those who have succeeded like to help those who help themselves. Great opportunities exist for pilots who demonstrate by their actions, rather than the size of their wallets, their dedication and passion for flying. You don't have to attend a fancy big-name school to get a good job. In fact, you might even find a job sooner if you go to a smaller school because some of the networking opportunities can be far better when you've got fewer competitors in a narrow field.

"Pay-It-All-Up-Front" Training Programs

Plans that require all tuition to be paid up front cause me to see a neon sign flashing "Caution, Danger Ahead!" Even the most well-respected flight schools can find themselves in financial hot water faster than you can say Internal Revenue Service or State Attorney General's Office. If you've paid for everything up front, you may find yourself at the back of a line of creditors if they close their doors before you finish your training. No reputable school should object to your paying as you go. If there's a financial advantage to paying in advance, limit your purchase to one rating at a time and check the fine print for the cost of extra flight hours, should more training be required than the minimums advertised.

One of our clients complained that she had used up all her flying fees before completing the required courses. Now, the school wanted more money to allow her to finish training. The advertised package price she had paid changed immediately into a high-dollar fee per hour when figuring the extra flight hours required. In this case, knowing what percentage of pilots had completed the program within the allotted minimum would have lessened the end-of-curriculum sticker shock that caused this pilot to spend substantially more than she had planned. Another client told me an even worse story about returning to his paid-up-front flight school after Christmas break and finding the school gone—doors closed, no instructors, no airplanes. They had vanished with all of his hard-earned training money.

"Specialized Ratings for the Novice" Programs

Many advertisements describe specialized courses that sound like official, career-enhancing programs designed to move you up into the big leagues upon their completion. Unfortunately, taking such courses at an inappropriate time, such as early in your flight education, usually does little to impress a prospective employer. Rather, it tends to reflect on your gullibility, branding you as an indiscriminate consumer.

It's important to understand what specialized training can and can't do for you when there's no experience or guaranteed job offer to support the training cycle.

Getting 25 hours in a Boeing 727 may seem like a neat thing to do, but perhaps they should pay you! The school may be using you to fly the airplane for a paying Flight Engineer Rating trainee who needs a body in the right or left seat to qualify his training time. Maybe YOU should be sitting in the FE seat? Maybe not. But the value of this rating is questionable and can lead you down a dead-end street when it comes to building employer-valued flight hours.

My advice is summarized by the old adage: "Learn from the mistakes of others. You'll never live long enough to make them all yourself!" Pilots have to become savvy consumers at the earliest stages of their training. There are many ways to accomplish your flying goals, and you should take the time to investigate your options thoroughly. Because the expense of flying can be substantial, consider training at a local flight school where you will save the cost of living expenses while getting similar results to those of highly advertised courses at a brand-name school in another city.

Compare costs carefully, visit your prospective investment site, ask lots of questions, and make a pros-and-cons list for each alternative. Then, consult a knowledgeable, impartial person who will carefully analyze your situation to keep your flying career on track and within budget.

Good Instrument Skills
are a Must

If you could pick one piloting ability that ranks above all others in importance, which one would it be? Super smooth landings might be up near the top because they're nice for the ego, but when it comes to keeping you alive and well-employed, I'd vote for outstanding instrument flying skills. Why? Because every phase of your aviation career can benefit from thorough learning, continual practice, and ongoing application of your IFR abilities.

My interest in instrument flying began once I had accumulated about 75 hours of flight time. At that point, I began to pay more attention to the pilots who talked in what seemed to be a secret language, discussing approach plates, ILSs, localizers, DHs and all the other mysterious details of another world of flying. The more I heard, the more intrigued I became, until I finally decided it was time for me to begin my instrument training and join the world of "sightless flight."

That was just over 30 years ago. I began working on my instrument rating in a Cessna 150 equipped with 1 Navcom and precious little else for radio gear. If I had known how important instrument flying would ultimately become to me—my lifeblood as an airline pilot, so to speak—1 might have had a greater appreciation of the training I was receiving. Learning the basics in a slow trainer with one radio helped me perfect my skills at a speed I could keep up with and saved me money as well. Later, when I was ready to handle a faster ship, I moved up to a Cessna 172 (and increased my hourly expenditure from $15.50 to $23 per flight hour!), which was—and still is—one of the best instrument training platforms available.

I spent many evening hours flying holding patterns as well as the FAA's infamous "A" and "B" patterns (found in the back of the Instrument Flying Handbook) in the FBO's back room, where they'd just installed a new Frasca instrument ground trainer. It occupied at least half the space of a real airplane, but fortunately cost a fraction of the aircraft's rental rate. I practiced climbs, turns, and descents repeatedly until they became second nature and I could then split my concentration to include tracking, turning, and timing. Later, when I started instructing instrument flying myself, I could clearly see how important good fundamentals are to completing the course in a timely manner and becoming a competent instrument pilot. Without these fundamental skills, the workload could easily become overwhelming and the frustration level insurmountable. So, when you're first learning IFR skills, pay special attention to the basics. They're very important to your future success.

> When you're first learning IFR skills, pay special attention to the basics. They're very important to your future success.

Using flight simulators to maintain IFR proficiency

In today's competitive training environment, some schools advertise total avoidance of simulators and tout the advantages of "all training in real airplanes." However beneficial logged flight hours are, they aren't, in my estimation, outweighed by the advantages of learning early in your career how to handle what will become a staple in your flying diet—the flight simulator, whether it's a desktop version or a 3-axis Level III Wonder Machine.

One certainty in any professional pilot's working life is the biennial proficiency check, which is almost always done in a motion simulator. Indeed, some type-rating training on new generation aircraft is now accomplished solely in simulators; the pilots never experience a real airplane until they begin their first revenue flight.

Although the ADF may soon be history, the proper use of any navigation instrument is based on an invaluable skill you'll need to learn early: the ability to hold a specific heading. Without it, you're constantly having to divert your attention from other flying duties to correct what should come naturally—good old straight-and-level flying. You may be annoyed by your instructor's constant harping on your heading control, but it's the secret ingredient to all instrument flying and the professional pilot's success.

As you move up the career ladder, maintaining your IFR proficiency will be an ongoing necessity. Many an airline or corporate job has been lost for lack of a good sim ride. In fact, some employers don't even bother with a personnel interview until after you've demonstrated your ability to master their simulator. Even if you think you're current on instruments, don't jeopardize your upcoming interview by failing to get some simulator practice sessions, including holding patterns, precision and nonprecision approaches, and partial panel work.

Staying proficient is much easier than trying to remove the IFR rust once it has accumulated. Even if you crank up your desktop PC sim only once a month, the practice is excellent and can keep your instrument scan fluid and current. The steep turns I'm required to demonstrate every six months in the sim can't be practiced at work with passengers on board, but they make for great training exercises on the PC flight-training device I use for review and sim preparation. If it seems a bit too easy, just crank in a bit of turbulence to challenge your scan.

Keep your instrument skills up to date.

The instrument training you receive to start your career is extremely important, as is ongoing maintenance of your proficiency. Even if you're not required to take a six-month checkride, which will hopefully force you to keep your scan current, 1 recommend that you pretend you've got a checkride looming and challenge yourself to keep up your instrument proficiency.

The penalty for rusty instrument skills can be disastrous. If you should fail a checkride in a sim, that's peanuts compared to the possibility of a crumpled aluminum tragedy, which can be the result if you don't maintain your currency. Sharp IFR skills can take you to the top and keep you there throughout your flying career.

Ab Initio Training

One route to an airline career is the "novice to professional pilot in just six months" course or similar variations that can range up to two years or more. All of us have seen enticing ads for such programs—often termed *Ab Initio*—in the back of flying magazines. But just how realistic is this approach?

Let's begin by reviewing what *Ab Initio* means and then see how it's commonly used in U.S. aviation circles. In true *Ab Initio* ("from the beginning") programs, offered by several foreign carriers, pilots are selected and trained right out of high school. The airlines screen numerous applicants and then select a few to continue with a paid educational program that will lead them to a pilot position at their nation's airline. Training can range from a few to many years of training and include a thorough education in all phases of aviation. It's very much a "many are called, few are chosen" proposition, designed to select the cream of the crop for induction into a lifelong pilot career.

In the United States, *Ab Initio* has erroneously come to mean learning that is accelerated or compressed into a short period of time. No funding or lifelong employment objectives are included. Such a course is simply a shortened or specifically-targeted version of a normal flight training program to prepare students for a specific goal. Usually the goal is to complete all ratings—Private, Instrument, Commercial, and Multiengine—as quickly as possible, often in four to six months. Some programs seek to train the pilot for a specific job slot after a normal two-year college stint, which may include flight training coupled with job-specific ground or simulator courses. Most offerings do not guarantee anything other than a job interview at the end of a rather expensive training program.

I've counseled numerous pilots who have considered such programs and several who have attended them. Most who attended had a very different picture once they had finished, and many wished they had investigated further before signing on the dotted line. Any major expenditure, particularly for a program that is supposed to lead to a lifetime of employment, deserves careful scrutiny. The old adage—if it looks too good to be true, it probably is—remains one of the great truths. Carefully investigating any expensive training program, even if you have to postpone your starting date, is good CRM—career resource management.

Time and again I receive calls from someone who's enrolling at Big-and-Quick School next week and needs counseling right now! To that person I give the same advice I give to the unprepared airline applicant who's got an interview date next week. It's much better to go in well-informed and well-prepared than waste the opportunity (or your precious savings or family loan) by jumping in without proper planning.

Is the program worth the price?

Pay a visit to the campus and ask some probing questions, not only of beginning students but also of seniors and graduates. Ask them why they chose this program, what other courses they considered, and what factors they felt were negatives. Have a few negatives of your own to begin the conversation. For instance, did they ever consider what their money and time could buy when spent at a normal-pace training school? And what kind of job opportunities await them at the end of their high-speed training, should their single-point objective not pan out?

These two concerns have to be the big stumbling blocks for special-focus programs that prepare you for a very specific job path. If there's a hiccup in the program or your own performance or the economy, your job opportunity may be gone in a flash. Are you sure you want to focus so narrowly that at the program's end you will qualify for only one slot, which the promised interview may or may not provide you?

For some students these programs are great. For others, they're a side step to the job-search problem that normally allows pilots to explore the industry while accumulating solo PIC time—often with no other pilots or passengers aboard. Gaining real experience by flying in unstructured conditions and making your own spontaneous decisions provides valuable learning opportunities that often don't exist in the canned, predigested flight lessons given to program participants.

The pilots in the "I can't find a job" set particularly like these programs as an alternative to proving their skills and resourcefulness. But big problems arise when the promised job turns out to be something other than what they'd imagined or they don't quite measure up to standards and wash out of the program.

Had they spent their megabucks on more training-type aircraft (more fixed-gear slowpokes rather than retractable speedy types), they likely would have accumulated double the flight time and substantially more useful experience. Even more important, those flying hours would have been interspersed with networking opportunities, especially with other pilots who might become their future employers.

Look carefully at your choices before jumping at the quickest program offered. Because we have no real *Ab Initio* training in the U.S. for our own citizens (other countries do their *Ab Initio* training here because the cost is substantially less), make sure you're aware of all the training alternatives before you leap into something that's often more advertising hype than realistic opportunity.

Accelerated Training: Is it for You?

Quick, quicker, quickest—these have been some promi-
nent buzzwords for flight training in recent years. During
pilot career counseling sessions, I'm frequently asked about
"quickie," or accelerated, training programs and whether
they can do the job as effectively as a regular, full-term
course. The answer, of course, depends on your situation
and the flight or ground course in question. A fast course
can be the solution to an immediate problem—for example,
you need a multiengine rating right *now*. Or it can be a
curse that is causing you a problem, if some form of quickie training has left you with no firm foundation in the
basics, thus hampering your future learning abilities.

Some options to look at

Let's take a closer look at options you should consider
before purchasing a new license or rating. First of all, look
at where the training fits into your overall career plan and,
if it's an integral pillar like an instrument rating, make sure
it will provide a good solid foundation in the basics. You will
be asked to demonstrate instrument skills over and over
again in your flying career. Each time you take a checkride
for any type of rating, your instrument skills will be tested.
It's therefore imperative that you develop good IFR skills to

> You should do your homework to determine how suitable such a course may be for your short- and long-term needs.

assure your timely progression up the career ladder.

A concentrated 10-day instrument course may work well for a busy executive who is tired of taking one lesson every other week and forgetting everything he's learned in the meantime. But, it may prove to be too intense for a 100-hour pilot who needs time to assimilate new material and integrate it into his expanding knowledge base. A bigger consideration is whether you have the time needed to devote your total concentration to this extremely intense teaching method. You should do your homework to determine how suitable such a course may be for your short- and long-term needs.

The IFR written test, however, is a different matter. Because the written test encompasses a wide variety of material, a two- or three-day written test prep course can help a newcomer by providing a good introduction to the world of instrument flying. Backed up by other learning sources—such as your instructor, reference books and tapes, safety seminars, on-line information sites, and just plain flying, the weekend ground school approach might be your impetus to start, continue, or finish up your "life insurance training," as I like to call the Instrument Rating. Just remember that the material you learn for the written part is meant to be combined with flight instruction and ground data from your instructor to make the material applicable to the real world.

The Multiengine Rating

A frequent candidate for the quickie school of learning, the Multiengine Rating can be accomplished in a number of different ways. If you have an opportunity to do some multiengine flying with other pilots, then it's certainly to your advantage to get the rating as soon as possible so you can log as PIC the flight time during which you are sole manipulator of the controls.

If you need a minimum number of hours to meet insurance requirements so you can borrow a friend's twin or rent one from the local FBO, you may want to get your rating in the same type of craft you will be flying; then you'll be that much closer to meeting the PIC time-in-type requirements once your training is complete.

If the specific airplane type is not an issue, look for the school with the best equipment, maintenance, and training available at a price that meets your budget and a time frame that fits your schedule. Keep in mind that once you're done, you'll find few operators willing to rent you a twin without further time in type. Consider purchasing some additional multiengine IFR training to complete the time requirements and, to get the most bang for your buck, complete an Instrument Competency Check at the same time.

Preparation is essential.

Remember that all accelerated courses require you to do the book work in advance of your flight training and show up well versed in the numbers for your specific aircraft. That translates into knowing from memory all of the limitations —normal, abnormal, and emergency operating procedures— before you arrive at the training facility.

Virtually the same advice applies to the Airline Transport Pilot (ATP) Certificate, which is actually an IFR checkride in a twin (or sometimes a single) given to very tight tolerances. Unless you have some definite reason for attending a particular school (perhaps they guarantee you an interview with their airline if you train with them), you can save time and money by taking an accelerated course, provided, of course, you've done your homework and have completed your written test.

Your home study will require you to be very current on instruments. Start with a simulator (PC, desktop, or whatever is available to you) and then move on to a single-engine trainer. Follow this up with several hours in a light twin to refamiliarize youself with basic multiengine procedures (particularly important if you're not current on what's required for this specific type) and then try to get some cockpit time in the actual ship you'll be flying so you can practice the various procedures and checklists before the Hobbs meter starts to turn. This kind of familiarity with the twin you'll be flying will cut your monetary outlay to a minimum and help you arrive prepared for accelerated learning.

By the way, remember that an ATP in a light twin is nothing but a paper credential that most airlines like to see. When you are checked out in the left seat of a large aircraft (over 12,500 pounds), you will also have to take type-specific training and pass another ATP-like checkride in the specific make/model you'll be flying.

There are other ratings that can be obtained by the quickie method, such as MEI (multiengine instrument instructor) and SES (single-engine seaplane). Be sure you've done your homework thoroughly before you take the plunge. Then, arrive prepared to absorb the maximum amount of knowledge in the minimum amount of time.

Simulators:
Help or Hindrance?

As you thumb through flying magazines, you've no doubt seen ads for flight training that describe the glories of simulators on one page, while on the next, another operator cries "no simulators, fly the real thing!" So what's best for you? The answer depends on your goals. On the one hand, simulators can be of great assistance, particularly in instrument flying, while on the other, they're no substitute for flying the real thing.

Advantages and disadvantages of a sim

If you're just starting your training under Visual (VFR) or Instrument Flight Rules (IFR), simulated flight time can help you become familiar with the instrument panel layout and location of various controls. You'll benefit from the time you spend learning the ins and outs of the equipment and can do some experimenting as well, trying out what each control does and how it interacts with the others. However, most desktop sims don't move, and there's a lot more to flying than just being able to manipulate an electronic box. You are experiencing only one dimension of flying. But the familiarity you gain is a bonus and can help you keep up your proficiency and interest when live flight training isn't available or affordable.

On the one hand, simulators can be of great assistance, particularly in instrument flying, while on the other, they're no substitute for flying the real thing. But the familiarity you gain is a bonus and can help you keep up your proficiency and interest when live flight training isn't available or affordable.

Keep in mind that simulator time accumulated without an instructor can't be logged, nor are many of the available devices considered legal substitutes under the FAA definition of a legitimate simulator or ground-training device. So if the time is not logable, is there any value to it? Definitely, and I'd encourage anyone who's got the opportunity to fly a sim—whether it's a desktop PC, a ground trainer, or a full-blown motion sim—to get as much time on it as possible. It's a wonderful training environment and can save a great deal of time and money later on.

I've had a PC-based flight simulator program in my computer for a number of years and find that it's a great aid to staying current on instruments. It's also a fun and easy way to practice various maneuvers and approaches, particularly nonstandard ones that you may rarely encounter in real flying. How often do you do 50-degree bank steep turns? When was the last time you flew an NDB approach to minimums with a strong crosswind? If you're like me, it's been many moons and your skills have waned since then.

Is a sim worth the price?

Although a PC-based sim program can set you back $400 or more, you may find it paying for itself after you ace your next IFR competency check (which can substitute at any time for the actual inflight hours and approaches required to stay current on instruments). Because you've kept up your instrument scan and knowledge of procedures by flying all the local approaches, your next competency check should be relatively easy—perhaps needing just an hour or so of prep to get used to flying a real airplane again. Very likely, you'll be able to eliminate some of the flight time you would normally need to stay current. After six months you will have paid for the sim by purchasing fewer hours in an aircraft to meet your currency requirements and you can continue to stay sharp on your IFR flying with a minimum of expense.

No one says that flying a sim is a substitute for the real thing, only that you'll keep your skills sharp longer and need less practice aloft if you've been flying your desktop computer. To save money, you might be able to share the expense with some other pilots and make a sim club out of it.

I've found that the sim is a great tool for teaching IFR flying because the freeze-frame feature and the ability to switch quickly from the instrument panel to the map display make explanations and such comparisons as "Here's where we are on the chart and what it looks like on the panel" a breeze. I use the cursor to draw a student's attention to the proper instrument or area and can teach more in an hour because I don't have to resort to hand drawings but can refer to real instrument presentations with adjustable settings.

You can tell by now that I'm a true believer in simulators. They definitely have a place in any training. How much depends on your particular situation. For those of you considering a career as a professional pilot, you'll find good simulator skills to be as important as the maintenance of your first-class medical certificate. In a word, all of us can benefit from regular use of a simulator, of any variety, because it builds confidence and helps maintain our flying skills.

CHAPTER 3

BEGINNING FLYING JOBS

Begin with an Airport Job

Working at your local airport, or FBO—whether you're washing planes, pumping fuel, dispatching airplanes, answering phones, or making entries into their computer system—can help you learn about aviation and plunk yourself right in the path of opportunity. You may know someone who has traded a ground job for a flying one. How did that person do it? How can you do the same?

> Weekends at your local aerodrome can be the most productive of all because most pilots and aircraft owners who work weekdays tend to fly on weekends.

Start by keeping your eyes and ears open. Adjust your airport working hours, if possible, to allow yourself maximum exposure to the flying public. Weekends at your local aerodrome can be the most productive of all because most pilots and aircraft owners who work weekdays tend to fly on weekends.

If your work keeps you away from public view, inquire about doing some public contact work on weekends that will bring you out of the back room and into the mainstream. There are lots of ploys you can use to get out and meet people. For example, planning a mini-fundraiser, with some of the proceeds going to a good airport cause, or writ-

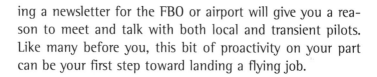

ing a newsletter for the FBO or airport will give you a reason to meet and talk with both local and transient pilots. Like many before you, this bit of proactivity on your part can be your first step toward landing a flying job.

Strategies that work

Take notes on new acquaintances, including how and when you met them. List each person's name, aircraft type/number, phone, business, and any details that might be of interest or helpful in your job quest. If you've got friends or past experiences in common, note those as well. Start a file-card system and attach their business cards, if available. Anyone who sounds promising should receive a follow-up call so he or she will remember your name and keep you in mind for possible job opportunities.

When you get your commercial license, invest in simple business cards containing your name, address, e-mail, and phone number. Make sure you have an answering machine, and please, no cutesy announcements—just a short businesslike greeting to enhance your professional image. Include the notation "Commercial Pilot" on your card and, if you've got your CFI, note which ratings you hold (Single Engine, Multiengine, Instrument) and any special area of expertise (for example, IFR currency, BFRs).

If you haven't already taken the ground instructor written exams, plan to do so as soon as possible. You can start with the Basic Ground Instructor (BGI) test, which will qualify you to teach Private Pilot ground school. Once you pass the written test, take your results to the local FAA office, and they will issue you the license in question, no practical exam required!

Even if you don't have the time or opportunity to teach, consider offering your services as a tutor to other up-and-coming pilots. Offer to teach a flying review session to any of the local pilot groups; they're always looking for educational programs for their monthly meetings. Regulations, takeoffs and landings, navigation, airspace review, neat new websites for pilots—there are lots of good topics for review. A universal topic of interest is how to prep for your upcoming BFR. You can simply paraphrase a good book you've found on the subject and bring extra copies to sell at your brush-up session. Be sure to include your business card and a brief bio with each sale. Or, create a program for wannabe pilots at your local business or health club. Advertise the free session and lure them out to the airport to your learn-about-flying session. Coordinate the event with your local flight school to offer introductory rides to those who may find your pitch irresistable.

More good approaches

The next step up from the BGI is the Advanced Ground Instructor (AGI) license, which will allow you to teach commercial pilot ground school or sign off a commercial applicant for the written exam. The Instrument Ground Instructor certificate (IGI) is probably the most useful of the three licenses. Because instrument flying is an ongoing learning process, you can find students practically everywhere. You could, for example, teach a pre-IFR class for new private pilots to give them an overview of instrument flying and encourage them to work on their instrument rating. There are lots of possibilities AND you can charge for your services! It's the old adage of "find a need and fill it." By the way, if you plan to get your Instrument Flight Instructor certificate (CFII), the IGI written exam is excellent preparation for the CFII written exam, just as the AGI is good prep for the Commercial written.

Although teaching ground school isn't a flying job per se, it can certainly lead to one. By getting to know the pilots at your airport and making your talents known, you've demonstrated your knowledge and competency in the flying arena. You may also find that several of your ground school students have use for your flying skills. If you've got your CFI, voila, instant customers. If not, perhaps you can negotiate some ride-along flying, particularly for an owner-pilot without an instrument rating or one who has a full day of appointments and would like the safety of an additional pilot for the long flight home.

Basically, you have to prove yourself, that is, demonstrate your talents and congeniality to a prospective employer. Make a list of your various talents and then decide how best to use them. Finally, talk to someone who has experience in your field and no interest in selling you anything but good career advice. Just remember that any job at the airport can be your key to an aviation education and more flying time. It's all in what you make of it. Perhaps you can come up with a completely new service or product. Use your imagination. Be creative—have at it!

Early Job Opportunities: Make Your Own

One of the best ways to learn about aviation is to experience some of it firsthand from the other side of the counter. As a new pilot who is learning the ropes, you see mostly the customer side of the FBO business and may miss much of what it really takes to make airplanes fly. There's nothing quite like some hands-on aviation experience to help you learn about the many facets of a rather complex field. Any public-contact job, from line service to receptionist, will allow you to meet other pilots and learn about the ins and outs of aviation.

After earning my private license, I knew I wanted to continue my flying education but I didn't have the money to buy another rating. So I applied for a job at a new FBO and told them I would take anything they had. It would certainly be better than the 8-to-5 desk job I'd been working to earn money for my lessons. Now, at least, I'd be out at the airport, able to listen to and learn from other pilots. Also, this FBO, like most of them, offered special discount rates on aircraft rentals to their employees. If I was going to build time toward my commercial license, why not take advantage of this important fringe benefit? Maybe the pay wasn't that good, but the excuse to hang around the airport was great!

An invaluable education

And so I got an invaluable education into the real workings of an FBO. I started out at the front desk, dispatching aircraft for the flight school, answering the phone, talking to pilots, and getting to know who flew which aircraft when and where. I let it be known that I was working on my ratings, and soon had various opportunities to fly along with other pilots and log valuable flight time.

> I found a friend who wanted to share flying expenses, and we visited every local airport to practice our cross-country navigation techniques.

Each evening after work, I'd try to do something aviation-related, such as attending a ground school class, studying for my written test, or flying for an hour to build more flight time. One of the local instructors volunteered to show me some maneuvers so I could practice them during my solo time-building flights. I found a friend who wanted to share flying expenses, and we visited every local airport to practice our cross-country navigation techniques.

I kept in close contact with our aircraft salesman, Dave Hemming, and found him to be a great source of bootlegged flight time. If his sales flights had an empty seat, I was there to fill it. This worked particularly well when he had clients in another city and had to fly solo to their location to demonstrate the ship. I also kept abreast of who was buying an aircraft locally so I could pitch my pilot services to the new owners, who might need a second pilot. By this time, I had earned my commercial license.

A new job opportunity

One day I found my golden job opportunity in the form of a local TV news anchorman who had been a regular renter of our school aircraft. He had just purchased a well-used 1960 Cessna Skylane and was planning to start his own film production company. I boldly told him, "You may not know it, but you need me to help you run your business and fly your airplane while you do the photography." To my surprise, he agreed. My new business cards read Pilot and Production Assistant for TeleZap Productions.

My next big chunk of learning included all the trials and tribulations of owning your own aircraft. Although the ship wasn't mine, I was intimately involved in its maintenence and servicing. It was certainly an education for me to learn just what it takes to house and feed an airplane of your own. Everything from the mandatory annual inspections to bad communications radios were my territory when it came to keeping an eye on N8466T. Insurance quotes, chart updating, IFR currency, tie-down ropes, fueling—I learned about them all.

And all of this had started with a job at the airport. I was friendly, outgoing, and unabashedly self-promoting when it came to telling our customers about my aviation goals. Many of my former coworkers from that FBO now fly for major airlines. The line boy, the front desk receptionist, they all got their start at the local airport, realizing the value of being where the action is.

Job Opportunites for Older Pilots

If you are an older person who has just obtained your Private Pilot Certificate and have an insatiable desire to progress further, read on. You may be interested in what jobs are available, so let's look at the case of a 46-year old accountant, wife, mother, and grandmother who is planning to obtain her instrument, commercial, and CFI ratings. She wonders if there is any hope for her dreams, to which I answer, "There are numerous opportunities if you're willing to pay serious attention to your flying and avoid the dabblers' syndrome."

If you really want a career in aviation, desire, determination, and persistence, rather than age, will be the most important factors in achieving your goal. Surprisingly enough, maturity can be a bonus as you hunt for a flying job. You will have to start at the bottom like anyone else, but you have a lot of history and experience on your side to assist you with the process.

As you begin your job search, remember that no one needs to know how recently you received your license or how long you've been flying. If you act like an accomplished, interested, and ready-to-learn pilot, you'll find lots of help and respect from fellow aviators who figure you must have more time than your logbook shows. Act like the experienced aviator you would like to be, and you'll be treated accordingly. Remember, you've got the maturity and skills to pull it off successfully.

If you're serious about getting into aviation on a full-time basis, you've no doubt considered some of the alternatives and have decided that now, even more than before, you want to pursue this avenue. Please understand that it's not going to be easy, quick, or cheap. You will need determination and persistence to prove you love aviation and are willing to do whatever it takes to stay involved.

> It's not going to be easy, quick, or cheap. You will need determination and persistence to prove you love aviation and are willing to do whatever it takes to stay involved.

Career possibilities

With that preface, let's discuss some of the possible careers. Flight Instruction comes first to mind and is a good first step to give you a saleable skill. For someone who really enjoys the teaching process, it's an honorable, longterm profession with many day-to-day rewards. If you're interested, one of your first moves should be to join NAFI, the National Association of Flight Instructors (www.nafinet.org).

Don't forget ground instruction as a good precursor to flight instruction. You can get started in the business with only a Private Certificate, once you complete the Basic Ground Instructor computer exam. Use your social and professional contacts within the local community to drum up new students for yourself or your FBO and use your new passion as an excuse to network and advertise your aviation skills.

Learning the ropes at an FBO is another good way to stay involved. If you have specialized skills such as accounting, computer, marketing, or sales, you might be able to widen your aviation knowledge by using your skills in an aviation setting. Begin at a local FBO and, when you've learned

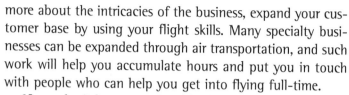

more about the intricacies of the business, expand your customer base by using your flight skills. Many specialty businesses can be expanded through air transportation, and such work will help you accumulate hours and put you in touch with people who can help you get into flying full-time.

If you don't have a marketable skill, plan to acquire one, either using the apprentice system or taking some classes to sharpen your skills. During my stint at an FBO I worked in customer service, accounting, maintenance, aircraft sales, and public relations. In a small FBO these are often parts of a single job title, while large companies will have separate divisions. Express your desire to learn each one or pick a field that interests you and volunteer your time, perhaps in exchange for FBO services, to get acquainted with what's required for each. And don't forget line service; it's the best place to meet future employers.

Aviation is very accepting of a wide range of ages. The common thread is a love of flying. You need only demonstrate your sincerity and you'll find many ways to stay involved. Yes, there is a great wasteland between acquiring your ratings and accumulating the time needed to qualify for a corporate or charter position, but if you're really serious, you'll find people along the way who are willing to help you. All of us have been given a leg up at one time or another and realize it's our job to help out the next deserving individual. You can easily be that person, but you'll have to pursue your goal actively and demonstrate your serious intent, not just dream about the future.

Becoming an Instructor, A CFI

CFI Ratings seem to evoke a love/hate response. Either pilots love the idea of teaching flying or they so dislke it that they will go to any length to avoid what they consider to be tantamount to indentured servitude. Perhaps the problem for those who hate the idea lies in the fact that they don't understand some of its merits.

I remember contemplating a CFI rating when I had between 300 and 400 hours and was flying a Skylane for a small film production company in Northern California. I really enjoyed the work but felt there wasn't enough flying to keep me happy. I figured a CFI rating would teach me more about flying, raise my confi-

> I figured a CFI rating would teach me more about flying, raise my confidence level, and improve my ability to fly an airplane from the right seat.

dence level, and improve my ability to fly an airplane from the right seat, which I knew to be the starting point for most flying jobs in a big airplane with two pilots.

I never planned to teach flying because I figured I'd make a terrible instructor, lacking the patience to deal with student pilots. Besides, I was more interested in instrument flying and thought if I could learn to teach instruments, I'd have a much better grasp of that fascinating subject. To my chagrin, I was offered a basic teaching position shortly after

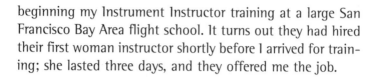

beginning my Instrument Instructor training at a large San Francisco Bay Area flight school. It turns out they had hired their first woman instructor shortly before I arrived for training; she lasted three days, and they offered me the job.

Plunging in

So there I was, teaching CFI students with the ink barely dry on my own certificate. In those days, pre-November 1973, they allowed new CFIs to teach CFI students without any specific experience. Now, FARs require you to have given 200 hours of flight instruction or completed 2 years as a CFI before teaching CFI students. The problem was, I had little or no teaching experience to pass on to them. Not to worry, said my boss, you know exactly what's required to pass the CFI checkride because you just took it three weeks ago!

With my new CFI ticket hidden in my pocket, I proceeded to try and act like an old pro and found it wasn't as hard as I thought. Because I had the rating, I acquired a lot of respect that came with it. No one knew how long I'd had it, and as long as I performed in a professional manner—voila, instant credibility! I just had to stand my ground when doubting students began questioning my credentials.

One particularly rowdy type, who tended bar at night, didn't seem particularly happy to have me as an instructor. As we began our first lesson, he looked me up and down disapprovingly and said, "So how many students have you taught?" I gulped inwardly and said, "Well, *here*, just a few," not wanting to admit that "here" was my first teaching job with my just-acquired flight instructor's license.

As I continued to teach, I learned a great deal about communicating my wishes succinctly. Once, while trying to get a Japanese student to reduce the power on short final, I told him, "Less power, take off [some of the] power" and he proceeded to firewall the throttle! Obviously using truncated English was a bad plan when my student had a minimal command of the language.

Special benefits of instructing

Instructing gave me a good excuse to hang around at the airport, learn more about flying, and network with other pilots, particularly those flying bigger aircraft. Instructors are always trying to find a way to break into multiengine instruction, as it is the golden-brick road to acquiring the much-sought-after twin time. Fortunately, I had several multiengine students but learned the hard way to stay alert when the takeoff or landing was in progress. One memorable moment involved a new ME student yelling "You've got it!" as we careened off the runway toward the trees—and me with no right-side brakes! Recovering my composure, I grabbed the controls, steered us back onto the pavement, added the takeoff power, and departed the area with my knees still shaking violently.

All instructors have both wonderful and scary stories to tell, but most agree that the learning experience is invaluable, particularly when dealing with captains in their future airline careers. Similarly, every airline captain I know will readily acknowledge the better job done by first officers who have worked as CFIs and who understand the learning process from the inside out. So, if you're thinking about a future as a professional pilot, consider seriously the CFI rating. You'll be surprised at its many benefits.

Getting Paid to Fly

Haven't we all been lured by advertisements shouting "Pilot Employment!" and claiming "hundreds of job listings for pilots?" Sounds great, no? Who wouldn't like a job flying for hire and building hours, once the ink dries on your new Commercial Pilot Certificate. But are there really jobs like that out there?

Instructing is one way to go.

In surveying some of the airline pilots I work with, I've asked many of them to tell me about the first flying job they obtained after completing their Commercial Pilot Certificate, specifying that it had to be a job in which they were paid to fly, not just one that contained some flying along with other duties. Invariably, they say "instructing," and most often qualify it with "at the place where I learned to fly," or "at the place where I'd just completed a rating."

Looking back on my own career, the story is a similar one. I initially worked for a small film production company but the flying I'd envisioned wasn't there. It was time to move on to a full-time flying opportunity, but who was going to hire a 400-hour pilot with commercial, instrument, and multiengine ratings?

Knowing that instructing was probably my only choice—and being very interested in learning the material as opposed to actually teaching it—I returned to my former FBO and completed my CFI. Shortly thereafter, I completed my CFII at a large Northern California flight school, which promptly hired me to teach their students. So my first real flying job was, like that of many of my first officers, instructing—to gain the knowledge, confidence, and experience that employers seek.

Building flight hours without instructing or without unusual financial assistance is tough. If you are willing to spend the money on an airplane to build time or purchase hours to meet the minimum requirements of most Part 135 air taxi operators (500 VFR and 1200 IFR), you may be able to schmooze your way into a noninstructing job. But quite frankly, most of these jobs are the rewards given to CFIs who work hard, do a good job, and show they've paid their dues.

On occasion, we see someone in our pilot consulting business who has worked for a corporate operator in another capacity, as a dispatcher or a line person perhaps, receive an invitation to fly right seat on the company airplane as a reward for dedication and perseverance. Sometimes, having an A & P license and working for a company as a mechanic will net you the opportunity to transition to a pilot slot if you've stayed current and continued to upgrade your pilot skills.

> **Most first flying jobs are the result of hard work and lots of networking.**

Making your own options

Most first flying jobs, however, are the result of hard work and lots of networking. Just assuming that you're in line to take over an upcoming vacancy or newly-created position can result in disappointment and frustration when someone else gets the job and you're left wondering what happened.

What efforts have you made on your own behalf to demonstrate that you're worthy of that first break? Persistence really does pay off, and if you know someone who might help you, use your networking skills, your "Double A"—anywhere, anytime skills, as I like to call them—to make sure that person learns of your interest and availability.

Creativity and ingenuity on your part are needed to build hours toward your first flying job. For example, look for a job that allows you to integrate flying with another skill. Or when your regular job requires travel, consider flying yourself to your destination. Yet another way to build time is to routinely fly yourself and your friends to places of interest, sharing expenses as you go. Maybe working with a real estate agent who needs aerial shots of properties or a mortuary that needs ashes scattered (check with your state regulatory agency for any special licensing requirements) will net you the excuse to purchase all or part of an airplane, or at a minimum, some block flying time to keep building those precious hours.

Think of first flying jobs as "by invitation only." To get invited into the fold, you will have to prove you've got what it takes as well as demonstrate that you will put that invitation to good use. The jobs ARE there, but, for the most part, are well-hidden, waiting for hard-working, deserving pilots who have demonstrated their initiative, desire, and dedication to the world's greatest job: being paid to do for a living what you like to do anyway.

To show potential employers that you're the best person for their job, be sure you always project a professional image of the safe, thorough, conscientious pilot any employer would be happy to hire. Although first jobs can be the hardest ones to land, you can create a demand for your services by demonstrating your ability to do your job well, whatever that job may be.

Moving Up the Job Ladder

One of the questions asked most often in our counseling business is "How do 1 progress upward from my current CFI position to a cargo, corporate, or commuter job?"

You can start by selling yourself with a bit of personal public relations. Don't keep your aspirations a secret. Let other pilots and airport people know what you're looking for and approximately when you'll be ready for a new job. If it's a CFI job, keep them appraised of your progress on your rating. If it's a charter job or post CFI job that interests you, it's never too early to start checking out the possibilities.

Prospective employers want to see that you have built multiengine time as quickly as possible, so you'll want to have at least 200 hours of ME time when you reach 1,000 hours of total time. Begin now to map your plan of attack. Having thousands of hours of light single-engine time and little or no ME time can bring into question your advanced flying skills and your seriousness of purpose.

What are the possibilities for moving up?

If you are an enthusiastic, inventive CFI, there are numerous ways to move up the ladder. You can virtually make your own job by carefully looking over the marketplace and deciding which way you'd like to go.

Is there any charter work going on at your local airport or a corporate operator who might need another pilot? If so, get to know the people who work there and start learning about their operation, including who does the hiring and what kind of flight time this person likes to see for new hires.

When you find a prospective employer, take the time to express a sincere interest in the equipment they're flying and do some research to familiarize yourself with the company and their airplanes. Ask if you can ride along on deadhead or ferry flights with no passengers, offering to pay your own way back if necessary. Obtain a manual for their ship and study it with an eye to asking good questions when the pilots have some spare time to talk. Find out where you can attend ground school on their specific type and, if feasible, offer to pay your own way. Trained, enthusiastic professionals are hard to come by, so you'll be distinguishing yourself and learn a lot in the process.

Befriending the current pilots of a prospective employer can often net you valuable advance information on their hiring plans; they may know if their company plans to hire, when and how many. Or, if any of them have personal plans to move on to another job, perhaps you'll be able to apply for the slot. Hopefully, you've demonstrated your sincerity and interest sufficiently enough that a current pilot will be happy to recommend you as his replacement or pass the word on to a friend who might know of an opening.

Remember, hiring through resumes can be a difficult process, so if you are there when it's time to hire someone, you'll make their job that much easier. You're a known quantity, and if you are known for your quality—in appearance, attitude, and ability—you will likely get the job.

Make sure you look and act appropriate to the pilot job you're seeking. Follow up every lead you're given and report your results back to your source to encourage more leads in the future. Think positively and show that you are proactive in managing your own career progress. Your destiny is in your hands—handle it with care!

From Amateur to Pro: Crossing the Line

If I had to hazard a guess, I would estimate that the majority of professional pilots started their flying careers as recreational pilots, intrigued by the fun and thrill of flying. That first lesson certainly started my adrenaline flowing, prompting me to take one lesson after another until I figured out a way of doing for a living what I like to do anyway. Crossing the line from amateur to pro came about through my strong desire to stay in aviation, any way I could manage. Looking back on what it took and continues to take, three distinct requirements come to mind—proficiency, networking, and persistence—but not necessarily in that order.

Proficiency

Proficiency encompasses many areas, including overall aviation education, flying skills, and currency. Staying abreast of changes in the flying world should be easy. You're reading and learning about your favorite subject, right? However, it takes a lot of time and effort. You will have to expand your knowledge base not only by reading pertinent material but also by seeking information from other pilots to learn what you'll be encountering as you move into the professional arena.

Your reading might include these magazines: AOPA's *Flight Training* and *Pilot, Flying, Plane & Pilot,* and

Private Pilot. Look also for copies of *Professional Pilot, Business and Commercial Aviation, Air Transport World, Aviation Week & Space Technology, Air Line Pilot, Airline Pilot Careers, Flight International, Airways, IFR, IFR Refresher,* and *Aviation Safety.* You can ask corporate or airline pilot friends to save past issues for you. If you don't know any professional pilots, attend a local flying safety seminar and ask the organizers to introduce you to some at the meeting. Talk to instructors at flight schools, log on to aviaton websites, and post messages on computer forums, letting pilots around you know of your professional aspirations and desire to learn all you can about your future profession.

Flying skills and currency go hand in hand. Whatever your skill level, reserve some portion of each flight to perfect your techniques. If you are flying just straight and level in good VFR conditions, now is a good time to challenge yourself to some tight parameters. Hold that computed heading to within 3 degrees, limit your altitude excursions to plus or minus 50 feet, and practice precise instrument pilot skills, even if you're not IFR-rated. I guarantee that when you get to that all-important IFR training, you'll zip through the basics if you can hold a heading and maintain your altitude.

Find a friend who wants to share flights and pick a short cross-country destination. You can plan the flight as if it were a major cross-country event, precisely and thoroughly, preparing a good flight log that accounts for forecast weather and winds, landing runways, and traffic patterns, and compute the fuel burn requirements down to the exact gallon. It's a lot of work, but you'll find the exercise to be fun when you share the challenge with another pilot.

After you arrive at your destination and are relaxing in the coffee shop, score yourselves on how well you did and give each other a mini-critique. Why were you three minutes late to the second fix? Did you forget to account for the departure maneuvering to get you on course? Did your arrival include a high altitude look-see before you descended to pattern altitude? Plan your return to concentrate on those areas you feel need some attention, such as headings, altitudes, checkpoint recognition, communications, or ETAs.

Networking

As to the second essential, networking, ask yourself if you have been using your skills to benefit your flying career. As we counsel clients, we find underutilized contacts and networking opportunities. If you think your skills are rusty, read a good networking book such as the *The New Network Your Way to Job Career and*

> Don't pass up any opportunity to network, from attending a local charity event to volunteering at civic or social functions or taking a nonpilot for his first flight.

Success by Krannich & Krannich or *Power Networking* by Donna Vilas and jot notes in the margins as you find ideas you can apply to your career. Many aviation job opportunities begin with non-aviation contacts. Let others know who you are and what you're looking for. You may not know the chief pilot of XYZ Company, but your next door neighbor may play tennis with his or her spouse and can plant a seed that ultimately leads you to an introduction.

Don't pass up any opportunity to network, from attending a local charity event to volunteering your time at civic or social functions or taking a nonpilot for his first flight. You may just find your best contact is outside the aviation world in someplace as mundane as your neighborhood grocery store. Your goal is to contact people who can help you or know someone who can help you by whatever means possible.

Persistence

Our third attribute, persistence, is a necessary adjunct to the first and second requirements. Your networking results will be useless without a good follow-up system, and your proficiency level will diminish if you don't keep at it in a systematic manner. Do keep in mind, however, the difference between persisting and pestering. Structure your networking plan to include meaningful encounters with people you feel can help you and follow up with handwritten thank-you notes and progress updates by telephone or e-mail. Respect your contacts' privacy and limit your requests to reasonable, noninvasive ones.

Instead of asking a chief pilot to hire you when you may have less than the company's minimum requirements, find out what you can do to enhance your qualifications for a future position. If you have other saleable skills—such as PR, accounting, computing, or sales—consider taking a job, paid or voluntary, in some other area of a company if it will keep you in contact with the aviation managers. Look for ways to use your other resources to lead you to a flying job.

Persistence has been the key for many a new copilot, who not only just happened to be in the right place at the right time but also demonstrated, over and over again, hireable qualities through repeated contacts with the company that ultimately hired him or her.

To give our three-pronged attack real substance, make sure you look and act like the professional you aspire to be. Watch the way your role models conduct themselves and emulate them but, at the same time, develop your own personal style. Make sure you are well-dressed, well-spoken, prompt, considerate, friendly, and well-prepared for whatever your current endeavor may be. Demonstrate that you're the kind of pilot who will be a credit to an organization. Set your goals and then, through your proficiency, networking, and persistence, make it happen, knowing you *can* succeed as a professional pilot by taking it one step at a time.

Other Flying Careers

In talking with pilots and aspiring pilots about career opportunities, we often encounter people who are thinking about a career as a corporate or airline pilot. In an attempt to give them a good overview of what they can expect, we ask them to describe their vision of those jobs to see what expectations they have for their aviation future.

One client we counseled waxed poetic for several pages about his goals to fly for the airlines or become a corporate pilot. He ended his epic with the remark that he needed to be home with his family at least four or five nights each week. After reading that comment, we suggested he look at some alternatives because major airline flying could not guarantee his homebody yearnings. If you have a fixed requirement or a quirk in your background, such as a major accident or violation in your flying history, you may want to consider some other options that offer more leeway in lifestyle and hiring requirements.

Career alternatives

Perhaps you're just not suited to the typical lifestyle of a pilot with a regional or major airline and would like to combine some of your other skills with flying. These may include sales, public relations, management training/consulting, travel, accounting, teaching, or any other job in which you can utilize an airplane to easily and quickly reach a number of job

> Anything is possible with some imagination on your part and good, old-fashioned hard work.

sites. Or maybe you would like to try something completely new in which an airplane or helicopter could be used to reach new clients or demonstrate new products. Anything is possible with some imagination on your part and good, old-fashioned hard work.

This type of employment could be a reality for you if you own an airplane or can justify the renting or leasing of one. Start by investigating the company you would like to represent. Maybe a few hours of volunteer labor at their offices, getting to know their product and personnel, would give you an insight into how they operate and allow you to formulate a good sales plan. With an idea properly presented, you may be on your way to flying and selling, or flying and accounting, or flying and consulting, or flying and—you fill in the blank.

During my early flight training, 1 recall meeting several salesmen from local aircraft distributors and aviation-supply companies who flew around the state, visiting various FBOs who purchased their products. They delivered orders and demonstrated products—often the airplane they were flying that day—as an adjunct to their primary role of company salesmen. 1 remember looking at their jobs with some envy, while thinking how great it would be to use an airplane in my everyday job.

After finishing my Commercial and Instrument ratings, 1 sold my skills to a pilot who owned an airplane and needed, 1 felt, a good production assistant and corporate pilot for his small film production business. 1 showed him how my skills could complement his new business venture and allow him to make his day more productive. Using my organizational talents, my ability to adapt quickly and, most importantly, my piloting skills, his business would grow and prosper.

Finding a need and filling it

If working for one company doesn't net you enough fly-ing, consider finding several companies that need trans-portation for their executives and promote the idea of shared airplane ownership for those with similar travel requirements. You'll have to research thoroughly the travel needs of each group and see where you can coordinate flights to common destinations to save money and effec-tively utilize an airplane. This concept has been the basis for the fractional system of airplane ownership, used successful-ly by turboprop and jet operators who can't justify the pur-chase of a whole aircraft, but find it makes good business sense to split an airplane with four or eight other owners.

Look around your city, county, or region and determine what's missing. How could you use an airplane and get paid to do it in the process? One of our clients who owned a bicycle shop asked us how he could build flight time. We suggested he look into a fly/bike program to be offered to FBOs who wanted to offer bicycle rentals to their fly-in cus-tomers but didn't want to be bothered with the hassle of purchasing and maintaining the equipment. With a proper-sized aircraft, he could deliver the bikes to each FBO, serv-ice and maintain them weekly, combining his ground and airborne skills into one unique, lucrative business.

Any make-your-own flying job will require a lot of leg-work on your part. But assistance is available. Your search for a pilot job can begin with all the aircraft owners you know and then move on to anyone who bases an airplane at nearby airports. You can get a list of owners from the local tax roles, the airport authority, or the AOPA and then contact each owner to discuss what services you could pro-vide. Getting to know your target personally is always a good way to advance your cause—and, at the same time, meet some interesting pilots and aircraft owners.

Whatever route you choose, make sure you've done a thorough research job before you present the idea to your prospect. And remember that any plan for utilizing an aircraft must remain flexible. Also, whether you're scattering ashes, making medical sample deliveries, testing aircraft for a local avionics shop, ferrying ships or owners to and from paint or overhaul shops, or flying traffic or environmental watch flights, make sure you conduct yourself in a professional manner, offering quality work and good local references. Keeping safety as your goal, you will find numerous alternatives to the classic flying jobs that can provide you with interesting flying that constantly challenges your skills as a professional aviator.

Career Choices: Making the Right Moves

Should I attend this school or that one, accept this corporate job or the regional one, upgrade to get PIC time or fly the bigger equipment that's Part 121? The pilot profession is filled with many such deceptively simple choices. Making the *right* decision can affect your future career path, lifestyle, and overall earnings.

Too often, pilots rely on poor advice from unreliable or uninformed sources when making a decision that can alter the outcome of their flying career. Or they place excessive importance on factors that should be considered but only deserve a fraction of the weight they give them in the decision-making process.

> How you make your choice and why you decide on a specific alternative is something you'll likely have to describe in detail to a future airline interviewer.

Making a choice is not the only important part of the equation. How you make your choice and why you decide on a specific alternative is something you'll likely have to describe in detail to a future airline interviewer who will want to know about your ability to make decisions and solve problems. So let's consider some of those typical quandaries we listed above with an eye toward how you would explain your decisions to a knowledgeable listener.

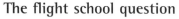

The flight school question

Choosing a flight school is certainly worthy of significant time and effort on your part. Just remember that what is advertised, often in fancy 4-color brochures, is just that—advertising. It's meant to attract novices and sell them a product. You must determine if you need that specific product, packaged as they have presented it, given your own education, finances, and geographic and family situation.

As you look at various options, learn what each school has to offer, compare its courses with what others offer, and find out what people who have attended these schools think of their experiences. Then, looking carefully at your own situation, determine if this product is right for you.

You should consider all the costs involved, not just those for flight training. Consider, as well, the specific contents of the program and exactly what you'll have when you've completed it. Remember that most schools offer the same FAA licenses, and it's unlikely that an airline, interviewing you 2,000 to 3,000 flight hours later, will have any significant interest in where you obtained your primary training or whether it was via a Part 61 or Part 141 training curriculum. They will be more concerned with your total flight time and the specific details of your most recent flying job.

The job question

As we move on to the job question—and consider yourself lucky when you reach the stage where this choice must be made—you'll be using similar qualifiers to help you make a decision. What are the pay scales, equipment sizes, domiciles, flight frequencies, and upgrade possibilities available at a prospective employer? Have you talked with employees there to see what they prefer and why? Finding out why someone else made the choice can often help shed light on an area you haven't considered. What will be the long-range impact of your choice, and is it a rational one for someone with your specific needs and goals?

All too often we see eager pilots jumping into a training program or job without carefully considering how that choice will benefit their own career progress. One pilot we know chose to leave a failing commuter line to fly corporate in his hometown. Soon afterward, his application and successful interview at a major airline had to be shelved because he did not meet their turbine-flight time requirements. Unfortunately, his new job involved less actual flying and he would now be accumulating flight hours to meet that major airline's minimum at a much slower rate. Had he waited until the commuter's demise, his total hours might have been just what he needed to cinch that jet job he wanted so badly. The choice is particularly tough when you're faced with unemployment and accepting a lifeline job can seem to be a golden opportunity.

Sometimes a slower program or less glamorous job may be the better choice if it provides you with some networking or stability options that will benefit you later in your career. I like to use my favorite "how will it sound at the hearing" question to try to determine if my course of action sounds reasonable to someone who is not intimately involved but who understands the business. Can you make a good case for why you chose to do what you did? Can you describe, in detail, how you went about making your choices to demonstrate your understanding of the factors involved as well as your good common sense and decision-making abilities?

Upgrading

Our final career decision concerns the advisability of upgrading to the left seat to gain PIC time versus flying as SIC on a new-generation regional jet. This may be the most difficult decision of all because major airlines often hire regional First Officers with minimal PIC time. You may not need the upgrade to enhance your qualifications, particularly if you'll be spending your days as a jet SIC, waiting for scheduling to call you and flying relatively few hours per month. Here's a case where some careful analysis and perhaps an independent evaluation of your overall flight experience might prove invaluable in helping you make an appropriate choice based on several important considerations for the future.

Plan now for the inevitable line of questioning aimed at learning about your ability to make choices. Think about how you make decisions, what factors you consider, who you consult, as well as how and where you gather data in order to arrive at your final decision. Describe your decision-making skills with a thoughtful reply that shows your ability to consider all options, weigh each alternative carefully, and, after gathering the necessary data, make an informed decision using good CRM techniques.

Building Quality Flight Time

It's the "Catch 22" of aviation—you can't get a good flying job without a sufficient number of hours, yet it's difficult to accumulate the hours you need without a job that allows you to build them. Until the demand for pilots far outweighs the supply, this twist of fate will surely remain with us. So what's a pilot to do?

Much has been written on how to build flight time, exploring paths from flight instruction to banner towing to wing-walking. Rather than review what's probably old news to you, I'd like to emphasize quality as the determining factor; you should acquire flight time that can do you the most good rather than just filling spaces in your logbook.

Isn't all flight time valuable? Well, yes and no. For example, a pilot with 11,000 hours total time certainly had the quantity required, but unfortunately for him, the quality was somewhat lacking because only 50 of those hours were in multiengine airplanes. The regional airline he hoped to work for noted both his lack of total twin time as well as twin currency and suggested he reapply when he could show recent experience in line with their stated minimum of 300 hours ME time. That being his goal, he returned some six months later with the requisite time and was hired.

Another pilot queried us about her 1,800 total flight hours, 1,700 of which were multiengine Second-in-Command (SIC) time, not understanding why she'd been ignored by most airlines to which she'd applied. We pointed out that with only 100 hours Pilot-In-Command (PIC), quality of flight time was the issue. Airlines hire captains, not permanent first officers, and they need to know that you have the skills to successfully upgrade based on your prior experience. With very little PIC time, her ability to command an airplane was a question in their minds.

The importance of multiengine and PIC

Once you've accumulated 1,000 or so hours of total flight time, you should ideally have accumulated at least 100 and preferably 200 hours of multiengine time. It's a tough and expensive process, but early planning as to how you'll acquire the time in a systematic manner can make the job easier and ensure your flight time will be counted toward an airline's total hiring requirement.

> It's a tough and expensive process, but early planning as to how you'll acquire the time in a systematic manner can make the job easier and ensure your flight time will be counted.

Often, the 500-hour pilot with 245 ME will have a better shot at a regional FO slot than one with 1,000 hours of total time and 175 ME. Quality can make up for quantity if you demonstrate that you also possess the maturity and judgment of a more experienced pilot. But don't make the mistake, as one pilot did, of assuming that just because he could log his right seat safety pilot ME time as PIC, that an airline would consider it as such. They felt that without his hands-on control, it was basically useless time, and gave him only 50 percent credit for the 100-hour package he had purchased at a time-building FBO.

However, don't change your way of logging flight time just to please an airline, as did one UAL hopeful. Check the FARs to determine the proper way to log PIC time that may be questioned later on. If it's legal to log it as PIC, then by all means do so. Remember that your logs may be inspected by future employers, all with varying flight time requirements. There's no reason to exclude FAA-qualified hours from your permanent record just because a potential employer won't let you count them toward their own special requirements for accepting PIC time. Instead, learn their definition and, if necessary, use a separate column to keep track of a special-interest item.

Build time specifically toward your goals.

As you build flight time, be sure that your experience is varied and will help you achieve your future goals. If your dream is to become an Alaskan bush pilot, concentrate on tail-dragger time and mountain landings. Airline bound? Then understand that chasing bush jobs in backwoods locales won't give you the radio skills and instrument proficiency needed to operate safely and confidently in the high-density traffic areas into which most airlines fly.

Teaching flying can net you some very useful skills. Often, when I counsel new pilot clients who lack interest in becoming CFIs to help build time, I point out that airlines hire pilots into the right rather than left seat, and some experience in this area would be very beneficial to their ultimate goal. Even if you never instruct, having the rating teaches you an enormous amount about professional aviation that would take many years to acquire in normal recreational flying. Personal experience has proven to me that most former CFIs make superior first officers, having acquired patience, persistence, and the ability to pay attention to details to make sure the job gets done right.

Whatever your goal, planning each step carefully will help you achieve it in the minimum time with the fewest wasted steps. Consider completing your advanced ratings in a twin, to build ME time at what's basically half-price. Don't, however, neglect to get a single-engine rating on your Commercial, should you decide to get your initial

Private or Commercial license in a twin. Expecting to fly multiengine ships all the time is a surefire prescription for disappointment in the employment arena because employers will frown at your lack of basic qualifications.

Flying to places you've never been before is important because the process requires careful flight planning and weather interpretation. If your PIC time reflects experience in instrument, cross country, and high-density traffic flying, not just repeated round trips to comfortable nearby airports, you'll find chief pilots taking your resume seriously. As you accumulate more quality time, update your file every 50 hours or more to let them know you're actively flying, are a current job seeker, and are eager to work for their company.

Keep in mind that you can get a flying job with the right kind of flight time. Determine the type of flying hours that will do you the most good, given your particular situation. Then, using all of your cockpit resource management (CRM) skills, consider all the possible alternatives before you undertake any course of action that will affect your future flying career. If the decision requires some major concessions, seek professional input to ensure a successful result.

Chapter 4

WOMEN'S ISSUES

Relationships and Your Airline Career

How does a woman successfully manage a professional pilot's career with a relationship or marriage? We know that the effort can put a great deal of stress on all three of you—the relationship, your career, and you—and all three can suffer or prosper, depending on how you handle each one. However, it is possible for your working and personal lives to function smoothly, just as they do for your male counterparts.

As you begin your aviation career, you will have to convince your superiors and co-workers that you're serious about flying. And you will be facing the dual problem of

Work to establish a conscientious attitude that's based on a thorough understanding of your job and a willingness to learn from everyone.

wanting to be accepted as a pilot on the one hand and as a woman on the other. Acceptance is possible without asking for special considerations or trying to act like one of the boys if you adopt the professional woman approach. This requires that you maintain high standards in both your flying and interactions with other pilots and avoid the games of one-upmanship so pervasive in male-dominated workplaces. Work to establish a conscientious attitude that's

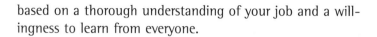

based on a thorough understanding of your job and a will-ingness to learn from everyone.

Should you act like one of the boys?

Although it may be tempting to jump into a lively ses-sion of telling hanger tales, you don't have to participate in every round of pilot repartee. Silence and a raised eyebrow can often earn you more respect than trying to partake in some rather questionable conversations.

If you find yourself in an uncomfortable situation, sim-ply walk away. You'll find that you command the utmost respect when you don't allow yourself to be drawn into any competition, verbal or social, which may have unforseen consequences. Mentally chalk up those times to the theory that "boys will be boys" and remember that you'll not change the outcome by joining the fray.

Focus your efforts in more profitable directions. When the going gets rough, control your own environment by finding a profitable substitute to occupy your time. You'll find a good book or article can easily fill the void and pro-vide you with an easy way to exit gracefully from an unpleasant social situation. I like to keep plenty of reading material with me at all times, particularly when travelling. I'll save a favorite aviation magazine for slack times and read it as a reward, after I finish what I must study for an upcoming flight or checkride.

When should you ask for help?

As far as asking for help with physical chores you can't manage, don't be shy. But be sure you've first made a good attempt to handle the situation yourself. I can recall fre-quently having trouble with a stiff oil cap on an Aztec I flew for my ATP checkride. I realized that getting proper leverage on the stubborn dipstick holder was part of my problem. So, in addition to tapping it with the bottom of my wooden shoe (which I also wore to make the engine-out maneuvers easier when I had to hold lots of rudder pressure) to loosen the threads, I made sure I had a stepstool handy to increase my ability to exert the proper twist on that confounded oil cap.

Secrets to success include having the proper equipment for each job so you'll be regarded as a resourceful pilot who makes a serious attempt to solve problems. Then, when you've given it your best shot, use your CRM skills and ask for help, recognizing that you can't win every battle, and these days women are getting accolades for demonstrating the proper attitudes when it comes to resource management.

Being discrete, considerate, and sensitive

You'll find, as many women have, that aviation is a small and close-knit fraternity when it comes to dating and relationships. Being discrete and considerate is especially important at all times, lest some indiscretion come back to haunt you later. Regardless of how much you try to avoid it, you will be the topic of conversation among the guys and it's best to smile and ignore most of what you hear. Often the gossip is designed to elicit private information from you or engage you in conversation when men can't think of anything else to say. I once heard a rumor that I'd gotten married and wondered out loud what kind of taste I had in men, as I had yet to meet anyone I even wanted to marry!

Many men feel threatened when they encounter competent women, particularly those in their own profession who can immediately assess their skills and separate the wheat from the chaff. I've found the best way to handle the situation is to let men know you value their skills and talents and are interested in them as individuals—for who they are, not what they do. The self-confident ones will appreciate your sensitivity and likely reciprocate, perhaps becoming a new-found special friend. A button I once owned read: "Men of quality are not threatened by women of equality." If you're like many of my women friends, you'll probably find yourself looking for guys who are secure enough to

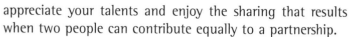

appreciate your talents and enjoy the sharing that results when two people can contribute equally to a partnership.

The real macho types will probably steer away from you, preferring to dazzle women who can be more easily snowed by their patter. It's just as well, because you would probably find the association frustrating and rather limiting anyway. The possessive types can also be very difficult in a relationship where they expect you to limit your range of action to accommodate them. You need your space, and if that means going solo, as far as relationships are concerned, so be it. Many women pilots prefer it that way.

Dealing with personal relationships outside of work

As you begin an aviation career, you may find you don't have time for a normal relationship unless you find the right type of understanding guy. Because of the amount of effort required to succeed in our business, there is often little time or energy left over to cater to a "high maintenance" partner. Thus, many women pilots find themselves single until their careers are well established, at which time they can begin to relax and expend time and effort in developing a mutually satisfying partnership.

Many men won't understand why you choose to be alone rather than with them. I think it can best be explained by the circumstances of our job. We fly with many males and we have to share much time and space with them in the cockpit every day. When on our own, we are often happy amusing ourselves and enjoying the peace and quiet. Being with someone is not necessarily better than being alone. We have learned to enjoy our own company and choose carefully when it comes to sharing it with someone else.

If you're already involved in a relationship when you begin your airline career, remember that it will take lots of tolerance, understanding, and consideration on both sides. You will have a lot of pressure to work hard and succeed as your job takes you away from home and occupies almost all of your waking moments. If you move your spouse or boyfriend with you to a new location, there is the danger of devoting too much time to him to maintain the relationship, when you should be studying and concentrating on doing your best as a new hire who needs to focus on the massive learning tasks at hand.

Remember what's important here and devote yourself to your job. You worked long and hard to get this far and now is not the time to lose your grip by splintering yourself into too many pieces. Ask your significant other to help you by accepting that your temporary isolation from him is a necessary part of succeeding at your chosen profession. It's important that you not carry outside pressures with you to what can be the most demanding period in your career.

As with everything else in life, it comes down to a question of priorities. If you're serious about this career, you must be willing to devote the time and effort required to succeed in it. You can juggle all the requisite balls at once, but to do so will take lots of compassion and understanding from both you and your partner.

Obstacles Facing Woman Pilots

In a professional hiring situation, female pilots are viewed a bit differently from male pilots. During the interviewing process, their skills are assessed in three important areas: technical competence, assertiveness, and gender awareness.

Concerning technical competence, many women underestimate the importance of being, as well as sounding, extremely knowledgeable. You have no doubt successfully completed checkrides where you had to demonstrate your understanding of a variety of aviation subjects. Now, you'll be judged not only by how much you know but also by your ability to deliver that knowledge in a professional manner. Do you clearly enunciate the important facts and offer a well-thought-out answer, or do you haltingly mention a few items and hope they'll not ask for more details?

Take, for example, a question regarding IFR Lost Communication procedures, a topic that must have all parts of the regulation clearly stated to demonstrate a thorough understanding of the FAR. If you merely provide a smattering of details, perhaps describing what route you'd follow and a transponder squawk, you've immediately labeled yourself as a technical lightweight, confirming a stereotype too many interviewers still harbor regarding women and their ability to handle technical material.

Instead, you should first summarize the answer by stating the various areas that must be addressed—route, altitude, approach concerns, weather considerations, and equipment requirements. Then go back and cover each item in detail. Recognizing your thorough, knowledgeable approach to the question may well cause the interviewer to stop you mid-explanation and move on to the next question. After several such competent answers, it's likely the questioner will move on to another topic.

> Recognizing your thorough, knowledgeable approach to the question may well cause the interviewer to stop you mid-explanation and move on to the next question.

Are you assertive?

Another area of major concern, especially if you speak softly, is your ability to be assertive, particularly in a life-threatening situation. Can you hold your own when the pressure starts to build? Will you be forceful enough to insist on the necessary safety precautions if a more senior pilot tries to intimidate you, demanding that things be done his way? Answering questions of this type in a positive, proactive manner will convince an interviewer of your ability to survive in this job.

Your assertive abilities will also be judged by the manner in which you answer even simple questions of a technical nature. Pay close attention to your tone of voice, your body language, and the confidence you exhibit in your own abilities. Avoid awkward pauses and ums and ahs, which can degrade the credibility of your answers. What I call wimpy answers may produce more questioning about your ability to do the job. Instead, sounding knowledgeable and confident will result in your being perceived as such.

Gender issues

Our last concern is your ability to fit in with a male pilot group. The male majority in the aviation world has little patience for "weak sisters," or those who solve every problem by claiming discrimination and jump at the chance to consult with their lawyers. Having a good understanding of the world you'll be working in and demonstrating your ability to work well with all groups is the key to quelling concerns about compatibility. Give concise examples of how you've solved problems in the past, worked as a team member, and dealt with sticky situations. Don't assume that interviewers will know you're able to handle off-color jokes in the cockpit. Prove it with a direct statement and good eye contact that shows you can hold your own when necessary. (This sounds like we're back to that assertiveness factor we mentioned earlier.)

If you're wondering, "Why don't male pilots get the same treatment?" don't waste your brain cells on this one. Remember, aviation is predominately a man's world, and most men are presumed to have our three concerns as natural attributes, unless proven otherwise. Given their larger egos and often excess of confidence, men will rarely consider the subjects we've discussed here, let alone dwell on them. Women, on the other hand, must prove their abilities in these areas to gain acceptance.

Recognize that technical ability, assertiveness, and how you handle gender issues will be of concern to your future employer and use this knowledge to your advantage. Impress interviewers and coworkers with your thorough knowledge of aviation, demonstrate your ability to assert yourself when necessary, and enjoy the opportunity to mix well with other pilots. You'll find that their concerns will miraculously fade away as you take pride in your accomplishments and demonstrate your ability to do the job well. You've worked hard to reach this point in your career, now relax, reap the benefits, and realize that success comes to those who enjoy life's challenges.

Perceptions:
Often of Our Own Making

One of the issues women pilots must contend with is their acceptance as serious aviation professionals. A woman pilot who was working as a receptionist at a Southern FBO recently wrote us bemoaning the difficulty of obtaining recognition for her professional qualifications. Male pilots, she wrote, don't take her seriously, and her boss just thinks she's a flirt. She found this discrimination to be very frustrating and, with most of her ratings completed (COM, ME, CFI), she wondered what she could do to improve her professional credibility.

Mary, as I'll call her, has a perceptual problem. It's likely that she's not getting the respect she feels she deserves due to the way she is perceived by her coworkers and her boss. On the one hand, we could tell her to quit her job and find a new one, but that may not be a long-term solution. Some things will have to change before she commands the respect and recognition she deserves.

Undoubtedly, many professional women have encountered this situation at one time or another. I recall working at an FBO that had limited opportunities for advancement. Feeling that I wasn't progressing toward my aviation career goals quickly enough, I decided to ask for a raise with the comment, "If I don't appreciate my own worth, who will?" I didn't get the raise but I did bolster my own self-esteem and went on to find a job flying for a small start-up film production firm that owned a light aircraft. I accomplished that step by telling the owner, "You may not know it, but what you need is me to run your company and fly your airplane!" Chutzpah? Yes. But I had nothing to lose and everything to gain, including a new, interesting job and a lot more varied flying time.

Altering perceptions

How you perceive yourself and how others perceive you are equally important. Women wishing to be taken seriously in aviation can have a particularly difficult road to travel if they don't understand some of the roadblocks ahead and plan accordingly.

First of all, women in aviation careers are usually in the minority wherever they go. I suspect that for every two who choose flying as a career, there are five more who have no intention of flying other than recreationally. Many male pilots have the misconception that women hang around airports because that's where the men are. This may be true for some, but for the professional woman pilot, it's a perception that has to be overcome not only by words but also by looks and actions.

So how does a good-looking female pilot get others to take her seriously? First, start by dressing the part. Dress conservatively and with an air of "I Mean Business." Try thinking of yourself as a corporate pilot who must appear presentable and businesslike for any situation. Wear a minimum of makeup, a fashionable but no-nonsense hairdo that won't be squashed by a headset, and clothing that is professional yet feminine. This may mean slacks or a skirt of conservative length, blouse or shirt, coordinated neckwear, a blazer, and shoes that allow you to function easily in various environments, from customer lounge to hangar to cockpit.

Conduct yourself professionally and with the utmost courtesy towards everyone you meet. If you're young and want to impress others with your maturity—after all, who takes a kid seriously?—model your actions on those who are doing what you'd like to be doing. Adopt a bit more serious demeanor, flash a genuine smile, and express your interest in both helping with and learning about all phases of the operation, including the specific needs of your customers. Your job is to make a lasting, favorable impression on everyone you meet.

Keep adding to your knowledge

As a professional you must direct a good deal of your time toward upgrading your skills. Strive to absorb new material daily. Read all the aviation publications you have access to and ask coworkers or customers for their trade publications when they're done with them. These may include *Professional Pilot, Business and Commercial Aviation, Airline Pilot, Aviation Week and Space Technology, Air Transport World,* and other aviation magazines. The subject of aviation maintenance, for example, may bore you to death, but having a cursory knowledge of some new developments may be the key to impressing a transient jet crew with your interest in their operation.

Carry something of interest to read with you wherever you go. It's a good way to make waiting a useful pastime. If you anticipate an available spare moment, put it to good use catching up on your reading. You will soon have the reputation of someone who is serious about her profession. And isn't that your goal—to be perceived as a professional who is constantly striving to upgrade your skills and knowledge?

Perceptions, both your own and those of others, will have an impact on your career. Assert yourself and act like the professional you aspire to become. If you find yourself in a situation where your talents aren't appreciated, it may be time to move on to another one where they will be. Or, to put a slightly different twist on one of my old sayings: "If you don't take a serious interest in your own future, who will?"

Dealing with Discrimination

I think it's safe to say that if you're a woman in aviation, you've probably experienced some type of discrimination, subtle or otherwise, at one time or another. In the early stages, unless you were actively encouraged by another woman pilot, you probably found few other women flying and often wondered if you were the only one with a passion for airplanes. When it came to flying opportunities, you had to work a little harder to be taken seriously. Too many men figured you were learning to fly just so you could hang around the airport—and them.

Eventually, you proved yourself to be a serious pilot with legitimate ambitions, but not without a fight. How many of us have encountered the current equivalent of "But you're a girl," or "That's no place for a woman," when it came to flying jobs for which we were fully qualified?

Needless to say, this scenario isn't new. Though I am happy to report that it's becoming a bit less prevalent, there is still room for improvement. Not long ago, I received a letter from a woman pilot who was eagerly resuming work on her instrument rating after finally finding a good instructor. Now, she was dismayed to learn that her search was in vain. Her new instructor claimed that his wife didn't want him to have any attractive women students, and unfortunately, she qualified!

This reminds me of the DC-3 copilot job I wanted badly so many years ago. "Oh, you'd have to check the oil and you might get dirty," lamented the macho captain. Looking back on the event now, I suspect he had no intention of ever hiring a woman copilot and only made the statement as a teaser, to make himself look good and perhaps allow me to think he might have considered me qualified for the job had I not been a woman.

But there's another side to this coin—the token-female-copilot—which is almost worse for serious women in aviation. This syndrome downplays competence for appearances and affronts all of us who value our pilot skills and feel we should be recognized for our abilities. Or, as my husband once told me, "You got your job because of your T and A—talent and ability!"

Countermeasures

The problems for women pilots are not all going to disappear in the near future but, hopefully, they'll become a bit less frustrating if we take appropriate countermeasures. First, don't lower your standards for anyone. This is the 21st century, and there are many sources of support for women pilots, including the Ninety-Nines (International Women Pilots www.ninety-nines.org) and Women in Aviation (www.iwia.org). Other support systems include mentors, both male and female, local and national women's groups, on-line aviation forums, and your own family and friends. So aim high and realize that it's not an easy road but one well worth everything you put into it.

Second, be sure you are well qualified and maintain your professionalism by striving to improve your skills with ongoing practice and education. One of the most impressive comments I received several years ago at a Women in Aviation Conference came from the Ninety-Nines President, Joyce Wells. During the early and mid-1970's, we both had flown out of the same airport—Gnoss Field in Novato, California. Joyce told me how she remembered me as being a "very serious and dedicated pilot." Funny, I never thought of myself that way, but I'm glad to hear others did. Perhaps the old "looks like, walks like, talks like, must be one" became a self-fulfilling prophesy. So take note and revise your self-image to include a clear vision of yourself in your future professional role, whatever that may be.

Third, continue to demonstrate that you don't expect any favors just because you're a woman. That doesn't mean that you can't enjoy and appreciate the actions and attentions of a gentleman. Courtesy and consideration are valuable tools in everyone's kitbag. However, you *can* be both professional and feminine at the same time. Because reputations are hard to shed, make sure you earn one that you'll be proud of and that affords you the respect you deserve.

Finally, learn to take the comments you hear with a grain of salt. Many of them will be aimed at eliciting a reaction from you. Others will be a lame attempt to talk to you when a fellow just doesn't know how to react to or approach a female aviator. I find that if I allow 90 percent of the comments I hear to go in my left ear and out my right, that tends to place them in the proper prospective.

You don't have to play catch-up or act like one of the boys to succeed in aviation. Just be yourself and stay focused.

You don't have to play catch-up or act like one of the boys to succeed in aviation. Just be yourself and stay focused. Your efforts *will* pay off in the end. One day soon you'll find yourself encouraging another up-and-coming female pilot, remembering when you were in that very same position.

How Women Pilots Succeed

Succeeding in a job world dominated by men can be a real challenge, especially for women pilots who are new to aviation. If you're thinking about turning your passion for flying into a full-time profession, there are several important areas to consider as you work to advance your career. They run the gamut from optimizing your performance with skills to dealing with gender-sensitive issues and learning to be yourself, rather than trying to be one of the boys.

Start by distinguishing yourself as you progress through your training. Make sure you are well prepared by doing your homework and reading ahead by a lesson or two so you know what's coming and can ask some intelligent questions. Show up early, ready to do the job. Don't expect any favors because you're a woman. Rather, show that you're qualified and sincere in your interest and enthusiasm.

Too many men like to attribute a woman's progress in aviation to her gender. The comment, "She is just here because she's a female" can be countered with a properly barbed reply like "No, I was hired for my T and A—talent and ability!" Let them know that you may get noticed because you are female but you got the job because you're qualified.

Some strategies that work

Networking, a major key to success, is a female talent that can accelerate your progress up the career ladder. There are several good books on the subject that can help you develop your skills and use them to your advantage. My favorite is *The New Network Your Way to Job and Career Success* by Krannich and Krannich, which details how to use, rather than abuse, the contacts you make. The "good-old-girl" network is alive and well, waiting to help you if you'll only demonstrate that you're worth the time and energy.

A number of gender traps can present problems to women advancing through what is most certainly a man's world. Rather than ignoring the differences, try to understand them and use them to your advantage. Learning about the world in which you're working can be very revealing, particularly if you can comprehend how men view you in their aviation world.

Since men do most of the hiring in this business, following some important rules will help you get ahead. These include learning the game of flying well and understanding the industry structure and the hierarchy of the players, as well as the importance of setting goals and focusing to win.

Women tend to see establishing good relationships as a goal in itself and are quite process-oriented. Men, on the other hand, see relationships as tools to get the job done. Said another way: women talk about it, whereas men DO it. Recognizing how the two viewpoints differ can affect your progress. It's crucial to your advancement to learn how to trade your talk-about-it traits for accomplish-the-job-now skills, so you're perceived as a pilot who's competent and enthusiastic and doesn't need special treatment.

Seven rules for achieving success

I could, of course, spend pages discussing each of these ideas in depth, but let me list the most important ones for you to consider.

Rule #1 Be goal-oriented rather than process-oriented.

Rule #2 Strive to work well with other women; they will contribute to your success.

Rule #3 Focus on one item at a time in dealing with men.

Rule #4 Use your power; that's what it's there for!

Rule #5 Be direct in your approach, particularly when dealing with conflict.

Rule #6 Remember that business is a game and act accordingly.

Rule #7 Hold no grudges (this is a particularly important requirement for women aviators).

Some tricks of the trade

In closing, I'd like to offer a few tricks I've found to be helpful in overcoming obstacles in our male-dominated world of flying. Be assertive, find a mentor, and learn to be a leader. These actions will help you overcome some of the many pitfalls that can easily overwhelm you.

Let 90 percent of everything you hear about what you said or did go in one ear and out the other. Much of gossip is meant to test your ability to get along with the boys. Notice, I said "get along with," which is quite different from acting like one of them. If you find yourself in an offensive situation, say so. Draw boundaries when you must and clearly state your limits, or the fellows might think you have none. No limits can lead to as many problems as having too many. You're a woman and there's no reason you shouldn't be treated like one.

Don't take yourself too seriously. Learn to laugh at yourself. Remember that success in this business is bound to incur occasional disappointments, jealousies, and rumors, along with many new experiences and positive rewards. Use your assertiveness, creativity, flexibility, perseverance, and courage to enjoy each step along the way. In a word, use your power wisely, it will propel you to new heights if you nurture it properly.

Balancing Family and Career

Can family and career co-exist in a world that seems to have no apparent regard for scheduling or lifestyle? Yes, if you're willing to give them the time and effort they deserve. Actually, there are three parts to dealing with this issue: you, your family, and your job. All are important and will require a lot of patience and understanding from the first two and some tolerance and elasticity from your employer in the third.

The trick lies in having the passion, determination, perseverance, and willingness to make the system work for you while not expecting undue favors from your employer.

Let's start by acknowledging your own feelings on the matter. If you're plagued by the belief that a woman's place is in the home, you're probably going to read no further. However, if you yearn for something more personally fulfilling and feel that your own personal growth can be enhanced through career advancement, that's justification enough to rank it right up there with your family obligations.

Family and career are not mutually exclusive. Both can and have coexisted for thousands of female pilots who are willing to accept the challenge of blending two worlds into a harmonious lifestyle. They find great satisfaction in pursuing their flying careers while also devoting the necessary time and effort to making their family lives a success. The trick lies in having the passion, determination, perseverance, and willingness to make the system work for you while not expecting undue favors from your employer.

Do you have the necessary passion?

Passion is probably a keyword when it comes to combining all that's necessary to succeed. If you don't have that "fire in the belly" for aviation, the sacrifices you'll have to make will soon become burdensome. If you don't consider flying a basic need, like eating or sleeping, you'll not likely inspire the help from others that's all important in this each-one-helps-one world of flying. Those who can smooth your road ahead must see your passion. If they notice this special something is missing, they will give their helping hand to others who are more deserving.

But passion will chill quickly without a lot of determination and perseverance to get the job done. The long and arduous training cycle alone is enough to discourage any "wannabe" pilot. Couple that with harassment on the home front, and who is going to bother to complete an aviation apprenticeship that often ranges from instructing to charter flying to night-freight hauling to commuter flying, and finally, if that's the choice, a job at a major airline?

To make the system work for you, you must understand its nuances and be willing to hang in there while it takes shape. Many men are skeptical of women's motivations when it comes to aviation. Tossing the girls some rotten apples as testing material is often their way of saying "fish or cut bait." You'll be expected to endure what any other pilot goes through, from lousy work hours to long commutes to many days or weeks absent from home—all for that "glamorous" flying job that likely pays $10 per hour.

Accepting the system

Start by realizing that none of these seeming career killers are forever. Being assigned to a base that's 3,000 miles from home isn't the end of the world, although at first it surely looks that way. Not leveling with your spouse will make it even more difficult, especially if you're now faced with a six-to-eight week training course leading to that undesirable work location. One pilot we counseled kept the secret to herself, and after it was too late to make any constructive changes, she finally quit the company, figuring she couldn't be gone from home that much with a three-year-old child to raise.

Her problem was looking at the job location as a death sentence rather than a temporary assignment. Initially, her airplane assignment should have raised a few flags. If she had wanted to make it work, delaying training until she could secure a place on an airplane that had bases closer to her home would have made more sense. And speaking with her supervisor would have given her some information on the options available. Not talking to anyone about the dreadful assignment was unrealistic and puzzling to her superiors.

The assumption that she could be gone from home for four to six weeks for training and that would be OK versus being gone from home for four to five days at a time for line flying—and that would *not* be OK is a strange proposition, indeed. I suggested she consider how she would feel if her husband suddenly announced he was accepting a job in another town and would be gone for days at a time. No doubt, she would accept the fact as a price her family had to pay; so why couldn't she present the same idea regarding her work location for consideration by her spouse?

Spousal support and employer flexibility

A spouse can be much more resilient once he understands your need to fulfill your dream. You have likely made sacrifices for your mate in the past; now it's time for him to cherish and encourage your own fulfillment as an individual. Making a career-minded woman feel guilty is a common tactic used to defeat her plans.

Should it come down to an ultimatum, make sure you're giving up the right alternative when you decide there's no choice but to quit a job you've worked so hard to obtain. Many pilots we've counseled were very sorry when they chose to give up all their hard-fought career gains, only to find later that none of their actions could save a marriage that was floundering for multiple other reasons. Ultimately, a supportive spouse is an essential ingredient to a successful pilot career.

Finally, don't underestimate your employer's willingness to work with you once your supervisors know a problem exists. Don't accept a job thinking the working conditions will be changed to suit you, but don't hide your needs either. Often there is a workable solution available if you communicate your needs in a mature, resourceful manner that says I'm enthusiastic about doing the job and want to find a solution that benefits us both.

As you proceed with your aviation training, be proactive in your own behalf. Speak up when you need help. Recognize that most difficulties are temporary and deal with them in a logical, systematic manner. If your goals are realistic ones and you've devoted the time and energy to them that is necessary, it's likely you'll be able to smoothly mesh your family and career and enjoy the benefits of your success for many years to come.

CHAPTER 5

MARKETING CONSIDERATIONS

Marketing Yourself: If You Don't, Who Will?

Throughout your aviation career, you'll find one of your main jobs is to market your talents and skills to prospective employers. This skill, though easy for some, seems to be one of the more neglected areas we find when talking with pilots about advancing their careers.

First of all, remember that you are unique and you bring special talents to your flying jobs. Even as student pilots, we all had something that set us apart. For me, it was the memory of telling a tower that I was going to make a 360-degree turn—and get out of there! Your job, as you progress in aviation, is to cultivate your special qualities and market them to your advantage.

How is your sales pitch?

Perfecting your sales pitch will help you progress through the ranks, opening doors that can lead to new opportunities. So how do you begin this process? I suggest you start by imagining yourself sitting in front of a prospective employer who is saying, "Tell us about yourself." This request is akin to their asking, "Why should I buy your product. What can you do better than your competition? Convince me that you're right for this job."

Start by making a list of your best qualities as well as those that make you unique. Your skills, talents, and extra curricular activities are pluses that you'll want to describe during your soliloquy. How will you assist their organization? What have you done in the past that qualifies you for the job? What new ideas do you bring to the company? What special achievements or awards in your past should they know about? Remember, it's up to you to share this information with them. Don't make them dig for it.

Organize your delivery into a two- to three-minute well-paced presentation that gives the interviewer a good chronology of how you got into aviation, where and when you accumulated your ratings, how you acquired the necessary flight experience, and, finally, how you happen to be sitting before them today. Be sure to make your progression a logical one, spiced with a bit of humor and leaning heavily toward highlighting your best accomplishments.

Did you work your way through college, receive a scholarship or special funding for one of your ratings, or score a 99 on your ATP written exam? Then say so—and be proud of it. This is no time to be modest, but do understand the fine line between bragging and informing.

Do you have interesting hobbies or unusual talents that don't appear on your resume? Now is the time to let them know you play the harp with your local symphony or once interviewed the President during your internship in Washington, D.C. Organize the highlights of your life into a concise, interesting short story.

Complete the picture

Remember, an employer looks for a well-rounded individual, and your job is to help him see you in the best possible light. Make it easy to get a full and complete picture of you the person; you, the pilot; you, their next employee. Often, you can volunteer information they can't legally ask. If you think it will help in the selection process, tell them about your family and anything else that would give them a deeper insight into who you are.

This should be an upbeat, positive presentation that gives interviewers the feeling of the real you. It should make them want to hear more about your dedication to and the sacrifices you have made for your aviation career. In a word, make your summary memorable—concise, complete, interesting, informative, and humorous.

As the interview draws to a close, you should have a prepared response for the final, "Is there anything else you'd like to tell us?" Plan to clarify anything you stated previously that might have been misunderstood. If you were at a loss as to how to deal with a specific question but now have an answer, deliver it now. Then, thank each interviewer for the opportunity to have interviewed and let him know you appreciate his taking the time to talk with you. Phrased in your own words, convey that you know you can do a good job and will work hard for the company. Finally, if application procedures allow it, send the interviewers a thank you letter, briefly recapping your visit to reinforce your application in their minds.

Remember that first and last impressions are the most important ones. Practice until you feel comfortable with the details and can deliver them spontaneously along with a geniune smile. Perfecting your presentation will help calm your nerves and improve your chances of landing the job.

Selling yourself requires some chutzpah, which you may not normally possess. Recognize the image you want to project and work to show that person to prospective employers. Each one will want to get to know you quickly in an interview situation, and you'll have numerous opportunities to practice your delivery. Plan your delivery carefully, add to it as you acquire additional skills and experience, and remember that your success depends on being your own best salesperson.

Career Quandary: Corporate or Airline?

As we talk with pilots around the country, some of the most frequently-asked questions are "Which should I aim for, a corporate flying job or an airline pilot career? What's the difference? How do the working conditions, benefits, and pay differ at each entity?"

You'll find as many different answers to these questions as there are pilots, but perhaps the information here will help make your decision a bit easier. First of all, keep in mind that one track doesn't necessarily preclude the other. Many airline pilots have accumulated experience flying corporate aircraft, and some (fewer, I suspect) have left airline flying to pursue a corporate career.

Both types of jobs are difficult to get and require a good deal of networking. Corporate jobs may be easier marks if you are familiar with the company you wish to work for and can court them in an appropriate manner. Airlines, on the other hand, hire in a more cyclical manner, and your application will likely be measured against those of many other pilots with similar skills. In a word, the competition is probably stiffer at an airline, while the corporate world tends to rely more heavily on who you know and being in the right place at the right time.

What kind of flying is involved?

Typical work for a corporation ranges from being on call (via beeper or sitting office duty) to knowing with a day or so notice that you've got a trip to fly. Some operators will give you a schedule of flights for the month, whereas others will tell you only your days off.

One thing that's common to almost all corporate flying is ground time (read: sitting around waiting for your passengers to arrive). Whether you're working for an on-demand charter or a company flight department, it's inevitable that you'll have to be ready to go when they are. The wise corporate pilot has something to do to fill the long waiting hours. For example, I found learning computer skills to be a great pastime that could be done while waiting, and the study provided me with endless hours of both entertainment and education.

The one big drawback for many in the corporate world is the waiting and the on-call nature of the work. As you become more senior, however, you'll find the duty better because the last-minute calls are usually directed to the more junior pilots. In the same manner, airline flying requires junior pilots to do more reserve duty, which means waiting for the phone to ring. You are, however, usually limited to a certain number of specific flying days per month. When the phone rings, it could be Minneapolis or Miami, one day or four—a kind of airborne destination roulette.

Corporate flying can be subdivided into different types of operations, ranging from one airplane and one pilot flying a single individual, to numerous aircraft transporting all levels of employees, to a situation where the top brass are the only people transported. (This last, by the way, can become a rather touchy situation when you're flying the person who can fire you!)

Corporate jobs can also involve much more than just flying. Your duties might range from cleaning and fueling to planning and purchasing to budgeting and acquisition of

> Perhaps the best way to describe the difference between airline and corporate flying is the "bus driver versus limousine driver" analogy.

equipment and services. If this variety appeals to you when compared with the airline's routine of fly your trip and go home, you should talk with someone who can fill you in on the good as well as the bad points of this much-sought-after lifestyle.

Perhaps the best way to describe the difference between airline and corporate flying is the "bus driver versus limousine driver" analogy. The airlines, of course, cater to the public's travel needs, while the corporate segment moves the upper echelons. You have more advance warning of your working hours with the airline's fixed schedules (in all fairness, some few corporations do schedule their trips weeks in advance) and probably more protection with well-defined working conditions and benefits. Corporation work often involves more perks in the form of expense accounts, Christmas bonuses, newer, state-of-the-art equipment, and a chance to hobnob with the rich and famous.

Investigate any job thoroughly before you sign on the dotted line. Try to get both sides of the story so you'll be prepared for whatever you find in your new cockpit. Remember that any job will seem wonderful as you start the routine, while several months downline you'll find your viewpoint changing—hopefully for the better.

Don't Let Glitches Stall
Your Career

During sessions with clients in our counseling business, we frequently encounter pilots who have quirks or problems in their backgrounds that have led them to believe there's no future for them as a professional aviator. If you are in a similar situation, consider some of the following case histories before you decide to throw in the towel. They might give you a new perspective on dealing with an interviewer.

A hero with poor judgement

Our first case is that of a pilot who had an accident on his record and feared it would ruin his future employment opportunities. This glitch involved a total electrical failure at night in a light twin. On first inspection, the pilot seemed to be a hero, having survived everyone's worst nightmare—landing safely with no power, except for a flashlight clenched firmly between his teeth. He came out of the event with a bruised ego and a couple of bent taxi lights at the military base he had chosen for his landing site.

With more probing, however, it became apparent that the airplane had a history of electrical failures, and he had exercised rather poor judgment in trusting a faulty component to function flawlessly during a critical phase of flight. Departing on a night IFR flight with one alternator inoperative might cause someone to question not only his good judgment but his sanity as well.

We suggested he stick with the facts, reciting them in a clear, unemotional manner. If further probing uncovered his error in judgment, we told him to agree wholeheartedly and discuss not only what he had learned from the situation but also what steps he had taken to ensure that this problem, or any other lapses in common sense, would not arise in the future. Providing additional examples of his subsequent good airmanship would help bolster his cause, demonstrating his rehabilitation and maturation.

A sticky mistake

Another pilot with a rather sticky FAR violation had a bit more work on his hands. Having landed at a closed airport on his first revenue trip for a commuter airline, he was surprised that the local FSS hadn't told him the airport was closed when he asked for an airport advisory. Perhaps he forgot that he was the PIC and certain responsibilities come with that job—particularly in revenue service. Reading the NOTAMS carefully to see if any apply to your proposed flight is one of those all-important duties.

Trying to explain such a glitch to another employer, after being fired for incompetence, can be a tough, although not impossible task. Your attitude, as well as what you've done since, can demonstrate your rehabilitation and how you've changed your ways to prevent any such occurrences in the future.

An unfortunate accident

Our last example is a tale of a drunk driving bust that should never have occurred. Our pilot was celebrating a newly-acquired CFI certificate with a couple of beers. On the drive home—after a few typical comments like "I'm OK; I can drive; no problem; I don't need a taxi."—another motorist hit our pilot. While the accident wasn't her fault, she was tagged with a DUI, ruining many of her flying opportunities for several years to come. It took a number of years for this incriminating evidence to drop off her record. Meanwhile, she spent numerous hours trying to explain the situation to prospective employers who were understandably skeptical of her abilities.

Beware and be aware

The moral of these tales is to beware and be aware of your surroundings and limit your exposure to any type of career-killer—animal, vegetable, or mineral! And don't forget that speeding tickets fall right into the same category as glitches. Employers hate them, figuring that your disregard for the rules of the road will translate into a similar distaste for FARs in the air once you're hired by their company.

One way to avoid such problems is to first ask yourself my favorite question: "How will this action sound at the (NTSB) hearing?" If you find yourself having to explain that you were in a hurry, or you thought it would work out OK, then imagine how bad this can sound to an administrative law judge who has to determine if you should be allowed to continue exercising the privileges of your airman certificate.

Save yourself a lot of time, trouble, and expensive back-pedaling by using your superior judgment to keep your exceptional aviation skills from ever being subjected to that kind of scrutiny in the first place. It's like the old adage—measure twice, then cut once. In our case it's—think twice (very good CRM), then act once (carefully and cautiously).

Fortunately, almost every sticky situation has a positive side that you can emphasize to a prospective employer to demonstrate your dedication. From violations to training failures to employment glitches to drunk driving busts—we've seen pilots survive the rigors of an interview inspection with the proper advance preparation. Many have overcome seemingly insurmountable issues when no one thought it possible and have pursued long, successful aviation careers.

Learn from the Mistakes of Others

Have you ever stopped to think about the immense amount of time pilots spend rehashing their mistakes? Aviation is perhaps the most hindsight-minded industry, and if you read its publications, you know that its survival, literally and figuratively, is based on learning from previous actions.

Let's begin by acknowledging that with the Pilot Records Improvement Act (PRIA), the ability to sweep an unpleasant or ego-crushing event under the rug is now limited. It's probably better that you now have to discuss an issue openly and honestly. If you do a good job of it, you can bolster your case by demonstrating what you learned from the experience. Avoiding the strain and worry that comes with the fear of discovery should improve the quality of life for a number of pilots who waste an inordinate amount of time secretly reliving their nightmare.

Recovering quickly from failure

Years ago, a pilot we know washed out of training due to lack of experience and expertise at the flight engineer's station. Much of the problem stemmed from his semiserious outlook on new-hire training and not realizing the importance of devoting every waking moment to successfully completing the airline's course of instruction. Because he had nearly completed his flight engineer course when the washout occurred, we recommended that he finish up at his own expense, using a local school's simulator, so that he could demonstrate his ability to do the job to a future employer. 1 recall that pilot moaning that he would never get another job, but his next interview proved successful, and six months after his debacle at one airline, he was sitting in the classroom at another. He had a fresh FE certificate tucked in his pocket, and he was headed for a new and successful pilot career.

A slow recovery

Another pilot—albeit with substantially less experience—had opted for an intense training program that tested his midlife career change skills. During his multiengine checkride, the examiner asked him to make a touch-and-go after rolling out from the previous landing. Having always practiced full-stop landings, the pilot reached over and, intending to retract the flaps, hit the gear switch instead. The airplane damage was minor compared to that endured by his ego.

Months later, after retaking his checkride and completing the school's curriculum, he was still devastated when discussing his major faux pas. 1 tried to show him how he could discuss the matter in a positive, "Here's what 1 learned from the incident" manner. However, try as we might to put a positive spin on the incident, it was apparent that a lot of prop wash would have to flow over this low-time pilot's wings before he would be able to discuss the issue in an unwavering tone of voice.

A failure that might have been avoided

Our final story concerns a pilot hired by a small regional airline who did not successfully complete the training—not an uncommon event but certainly a major impediment to his career progress if he lets it assume unrealistic proportions. The problem: ground school and simulator training provided little information on some of the advanced EFIS systems the students were expected to use. Just prior to his final checkride, the pilot asked for more instruction, but the request was brushed off with the reply, "You'll do fine."

Actually, the pilot did an OK job of interpreting the systems in question but blew another procedure during the ride, leading to his termination. To his credit, this pilot did not give up and accepted an office job at the same company while rebuilding his self-confidence and flying skills. Later, he was hired by a night freight company and gained some valuable experience that was lacking in his previous job. The problem here was a lack of assertiveness early in the program that rendered him unable to refuse a checkride he was not prepared for.

The importance of attitude

Being fired or washing out of a training program is not the end of the world—unless you let it be. Your attitude and actions are the keys to your success. Several pilots we know have filed lawsuits against their former employers to recover their jobs. In some of these cases, such a drastic step might have been avoided by legal negotiations between the parties involved. If you're looking to get your job back, it would be prudent to explore alternative solutions prior to proclaiming "I'll see you in court!"

Being fired or washing out of a training program is not the end of the world—unless you let it be. Your attitude and actions are the keys to your success.

Attitude is really the dealmaker in aviation. We've seen companies bend over backward to work with pilots who displayed an honest, sincere desire to do the job and work within the system. Being a new-hire pilot on probation, however, is quite different from having trouble once you're an established employee. It's important to recognize that your initial training is often an up-or-out situation. You must literally justify your existence and demonstrate you have what it takes to do the job. Don't jeopardize your position by underestimating the importance of towing the line, down to the smallest detail.

Your continued employment depends on a variety of factors: preparation, perseverance, promptness, and the big one, maintaining a positive attitude. Remember how hard you worked to get your job. Now, dedicate yourself to keeping it by learning to do it their way, asking for help when you need it, concentrating on your training with no outside distractions, and demonstrating that you *are* that exemplary employee they hired to fly their airplanes.

Mistakes You Wish You'd Never Made

How many times have you wished you could back up about 30 seconds and redo your last action? From flip comments to plain old bad judgment calls, we've all had occasions when we wished we had done things a bit differently. Hindsight, they say, is 20/20, but since we can all be a bit myopic at times, I'd like to focus on a few of the little mistakes we're prone to make and how to avoid them before they grow into larger ones.

A rather gross error came to my attention one day from a chief pilot at a regional airline whose company had undergone many changes during the last few years. One day, he received a pilot's resume addressed to the chief pilot who had retired years before while at their former airline's name and in a long-since vacated location; he sighed in disgust. "What's the matter with pilots these days? Can't they pay attention to details, especially important ones like who should receive their resume and where to send it?"

The sad part of this story is that this pilot might have gained an interview if he had managed to correct the gross errors before he mailed his resume. His qualifications were good ones that interested this chief pilot, but they couldn't overshadow the glaring blunder of not mailing the data to the right person at the proper location.

With today's preponderance of information available at the touch of a computer or telephone button, there's no excuse for botching something as simple as a name and address. Each company who receives your resume could be your future employer. Be sure to double check your details before you launch into your advertising campaign.

The failed checkride

No doubt the majority of pilots have failed a checkride at some time during their careers, but the reasons we hear discussed during interview preparation sessions tend to demonstrate the poor judgment of the applicant rather than unavoidable mistakes that led to their failure. Since you know you're going to have to discuss any failed checkride in a future interview, begin now to consider how you can minimize the damage such an event could have on your record.

First and foremost, don't take a checkride before you're ready. Never be too proud to ask for more instruction or postpone the event to adequately prepare for it. No one looking back on your flying history will know you took a little extra time to complete a rating or license. Besides, you could probably use the extra flight time, which all goes toward that important number—your total flight hours. A check ride failure, however, will remain on your record forever and be something you'll have to explain at every job interview.

Time and again we see pilots taking checkrides when they're not prepared or are overstressed or physically sick, figuring it's best to just get it over with rather than relive the anxiety and pressure that routinely precede a checkride. Here is where your good judgment (that nagging voice in the back of your head) should tell you how stupid it is to risk blemishing your good record just for the sake of expediency.

How will it sound at the hearing?

Every time I'm faced with a decision that could later be construed as less than sterling (read: stupid), I ask myself,

"How will it sound at the NTSB hearing?"—which could likely occur if my judgment is wrong and my course of action is a poor one. If the answer is "not good," then another course of action is probably wise. Rushing into a situation that offers no penalty for waiting is both stupid and immature, as well as a leading cause of airplane accidents.

Look into your own background. No doubt you can find examples of your own poor judgment. Hopefully, the mistakes are small ones you've learned from and can now use to help temper your future actions. In my own attempts to slow down my sometimes hurried nature, I've developed a self-imposed set of rules that says 1) If you have to rush to get something done, you're not doing it right and 2) If you take the time now to consider the consequences of your actions *before* they occur, perhaps you'll *not* find yourself wishing you could back up 30 seconds after you've done something that should have been covered by Rule # 1.

When all is said and done, perhaps the most important of all is my captain's rule: Look carefully at whatever action you're about to undertake in our unforgiving aviation world and ask yourself if you've carefully considered all the necessary variables. Is there anything you can change now, rather than regret later? Do it now, while you have the chance (and the consequences are likely nil). If it takes an extra three minutes to make sure you avoid wake turbulence or you have to delay 10 minutes to depart on the longer runway that's into the wind, just remind yourself that this is what judgment's all about.

You've probably got your own list of mistakes you wish you'd never made. Just remind yourself, as I do, that time is on your side. Use it wisely to ensure many years of happy, productive flying.

Acknowledge Your Shortcomings

"Practice makes perfect" is good advice when it comes to honing your instrument skills, but if you're getting many interview opportunities and too few offers of employment, you may be using the wrong strategy.

Most pilots think of themselves as skilled aviators but often forget that the art of interviewing involves discussing both good AND bad attributes. Ask pilots to tell you about three weaknesses they possess, and too often, you'll get a blank stare or a verbatim rendition of words they've read in some interview manual.

It's not easy to talk about your shortcomings.

Discussing chinks in your armor can be one of the most difficult and terror-filled parts of the interview process. Your weaknesses might range from what your friends say about you—for example, "Gee, George, you should lighten up on your days off."—to a short review of some personal skills that could use improvement. Give this subject some thought and you'll see that it requires you to speak honestly and with some introspection.

If your shortcoming involves a documented misdeed or mistake, that's a more serious problem, but in most cases not an insurmountable one. Accidents, incidents, FAR violations, failed checkrides, job dismissals, alcohol abuse, or driving offenses are issues that should be carefully and thoughtfully discussed, lest they become an invisible noose around your neck. In fact, there are some pilots who figure they're doomed to remain in their current job forever due to an unsavory event in their past. Rather than face the issue and discuss it in an open, honest, and mature manner, they spend years castigating themselves for these sins and never seek advancement or resolution of the problem.

Getting things out in the open

How you discuss a problem at an interview can be the catalyst that moves the interviewer into your camp and lets this person see you as honest and open, someone who has paid for past transgressions and is actively seeking to make amends. Remember that the applicant with nary a mark on his or her record is sometimes viewed as too good to be true, or, said another way—"What is this person hiding from us?" Having something that gives an interviewer a good look at your human side may be just the ticket to landing a job.

> Having something that gives an interviewer a good look at your human side may be just the ticket to landing a job.

Big flaws tend to rear their ugly heads initially on an employment application. How you phrase an unsavory event can be the key to getting past the first cut and into the "to be interviewed" pile. Never lie on your application, but don't scream out your sins when they need only be spoken softly. A job firing can be listed as "disagreed with company policy" and explained in detail during a face-to-face meeting. An FAA action can be acknowledged with a "to be discussed" or stated factually in an attachment, depending on the application's instructions. Some good advice from a knowledgeable source on how to properly present your problem can be worth many times the dollar investment and net you the results you desire: a chance to tell your story at a face-to-face interview.

Show up prepared.

Once you get the invitation to interview, begin your preparations by obtaining all the written data, both official and unofficial, that pertains to your event. This should include local, state, and federal records and transcripts as well as supporting information from knowledgeable sources, including supervisors, coworkers, family, and friends. Nothing distresses an interviewer more than to find the applicant has arrived unprepared to discuss the details of a wrongdoing and offers a lame excuse for not having the documentation that could have answered their questions and perhaps cinched the job. In a word, know what's in your official dossier and offer copies (one for each interviewer) of important data so they know you're not hiding anything.

Good ways to present bad information

Now that you have the naked truth available for their scrutiny, prepare your own presentation and discuss your problem in an organized, concise, and unemotional manner. Use a 3-step format of 1) setting the scene, 2) stating factually what happened, and 3) telling them what you learned from the situation as well as what you did about it. Practice your delivery so it sounds straightforward and unrehearsed. Include only the important points of your dilemma, offering more information should they require it.

Rather than waiting for the interviewer to pop the question, I recommend that you take the offensive position and discuss the issue as soon as you've got the opportunity to do so. For example, if you've been asked the classic "Tell us about yourself" question, weave your issue into your story so it's something you brought up on your own, not a closet skeleton they had to pry out of you. Often this up-front approach will totally defuse the issue, particularly when it's something that occurred in your youth (poor college grades, a failed checkride, a job dismissal) and you can now discuss it in a mature, positive manner.

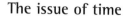

The issue of time

If your event is in the recent past, don't assume that you have to wait a prescribed amount of time before moving on with your career. The time issue is mainly for your benefit, to help you become desensitized and able to discuss it factually. One pilot we know had been rejected after a positive interview with a large regional airline. He and the interviewer had discussed the issue in question, but when the rejection letter arrived, the pilot figured it was time to do some penance.

Time had removed some of the sting, but here's a case where he mistakenly confused one negative reaction as an industry-wide standard, not realizing that each company would judge him and his transgression by their own criteria. With some counseling on how to discuss the problem, this pilot went to an interview just three weeks later and immediately received a job offer, pending a successful pre-hire sim ride. You can't assume that all airlines have the same criteria for hiring. And if they're short on pilots (class starts Monday), many recruiters will massage the rules to accommodate their current needs.

The bottom line is: don't assume anything. Times change and so do an airline's criteria. Your own outlook on what has transpired in your background may change as well. Be prepared with the facts and present them in an honest, unemotional, and upbeat manner. You'll find that your worst fears are often products of your own imagination, and facing up to them can help heal your wounds and move you up to the pilot job you thought was beyond your reach.

Job Continuity:
How Crucial is It?

Should I stay with my turboprop position or move up to a jet job? That's the quandary one of our clients recently found himself in after working his way up through the flight instructor ranks. We had counseled him 8 to 10 months earlier and at that time discussed the various routes available to accumulate the experience necessary to qualify him for an airline pilot job. Now, he was faced with a dilemma and wanted our input as to which option was the career-enhancing move.

Joe, as we'll call him, was currently employed as a first officer flying freight throughout the Midwest on a medium-size turboprop. He now had a job offer to fly right seat on a small jet for another small Part 135 cargo carrier. Should he make the switch?

Without knowing all the details, it was tempting to say, "Of course, jets are better than props." But after making a closer inspection, it became apparent that this might not be the case. It's always important to consider all factors regarding your current job and a future opportunity. These factors include type of aircraft flown, position held, advancement prospects, pay and benefits, company stability, working conditions, maintenance of aircraft, and, equally important, how a change will look in your own career progression.

Evaluating job offers

To help evaluate each offer, make a pros-and-cons list. Gather your information from current and former employees at both job sites. Ask those who have been there, both long and short term, what kind of background they came from, why they chose that company, and if they had it to do all over again, would they make the same decision? What do they like best about their job—and least? How much employee turnover is occurring at each company and why?

> Ask those who have been there, both long and short term, what kind of background they came from, why they chose that company, and if they had it to do all over again, would they make the same decision?

Our client was enthralled with the idea of flying jets and made the assumption that a job with jet time had to look better than one flying a turboprop. I asked him questions about the size of the pilot force he would be joining and how long it would be before he moved up to the left seat. How many hours would he accumulate weekly or monthly and in what kind of weather conditions? How did the pay compare, and did he realize that as the bottom man on the totem pole, he would be the first to be laid off if the company's fortunes waned?

At his present job he had some seniority and would soon be moving up to the left seat. How long did he think that would take? PIC time is invaluable, particularly in scheduled flight operations. (Moving to a corporate job, for example, just for the glamour of flying a jet, could be a dangerous trap—perhaps providing little actual flight time if it was not a scheduled flight operation.)

This job-switch decision could boil down to a choice between a relatively rapid upgrade to captain on his current turboprop or long-term stagnation in the right seat on the jet. All of these questions would be important considerations for his career progression in the future and his eventual hiring at a major airline.

Since he had been working at his present job for just over four months, the new jet position would have to be a great improvement in working conditions and career advancement possibilities to overcome the tendency of future interviewers to label this move as glamour seeking and regard it as job-hopping. Did his present company have affiliations with a larger airline that might provide referral opportunities in the future? Was one job geographically or financially more appealing than the other and could thus be easily explained as a logical career move to anyone reviewing his employment background in the future?

How will each move look to a future employer?

Making what could be considered a lateral job move entails lots of information gathering and soul searching. You should be careful not to jump at the first carrot that's dangled in front of you lest you label yourself as impatient and unwilling to pay your dues. Think about your ultimate goal and imagine a major airline interviewer, staring at you across the desk, asking you what you have done to demonstrate your dedication to an aviation career.

If you've always taken the easy way out and split when the going got rough, you will be labeled a lightweight, happy to reap the benefits of our profession without devoting the time and effort necessary to develop the maturity and experience that comes with some on-the-job seasoning. On the other hand, if you've done your homework and considered the alternatives carefully, you will have some good reasons to explain your move and its place in your career advancement plan. Later, when an interviewer asks you to give an example of your decision-making skills, you'll have an excellent example from your own background that demonstrates your ability to make logical choices after carefully considering all the options available to you.

Further considerations

Unless they're clear-cut, job changes can and should be approached with care. That's not to say you shouldn't move up when the opportunity arises, but consider carefully the consequences of your action, just as you would when you're flying. Use as many of your CRM skills as possible—including inquiry, risk assessment, situational awareness, planning, problem solving, and decision making—to gather all the facts before you make your final decision.

One employment axiom especially applicable to the world of aviation is—never quit one flying job until you have another, unless you have an ironclad reason for doing so. Circular files are filled with the resumes of unemployed pilots. You'll have to work twice, no, three times as hard to find another flying job. And you'll have to explain why you left your last position. As an added detraction, you will also have to explain that period of unemployment on any subsequent job application. A better solution is to consider each job offer carefully, research it to the best of your ability, consult with others experienced in the field, and then weigh all the options to reach an enlightened decision. Like emergencies, job decisions are best begun with a bit of "sitting on your hands" before you do anything you'll regret later.

Getting Back Into Flying

When times are good and the economy begins to pick up, pilots who have left the flying profession begin to wonder if they made the right move. Perhaps you are one of the many pilots who is thinking about getting back into flying but are wondering what it's going to take in terms of time, money, and effort. Is the effort really worth it? Many of the answers will require you to look carefully at your own needs and goals. Others will depend on how much you really miss the profession and how unhappy you are with your present job situation and lifestyle.

Water testers and reentry pilots

We have recently counseled people who earned their private licenses several years ago and, now that they're doing well at their present jobs, wonder if they should try to get into flying full time? Others have built up their hours to the 350 to 500 mark by flying for pleasure, possess noncurrent instrument ratings, and are looking longingly at friends who fly for a living and enjoy their work. This group, we call them the water testers, aren't really going back to flying but are resuming where they left off, with hopes of changing their status from amateur to pro. It will certainly take a lot of work, determination, and—let's not forget that all important aviation ingredient—money. However, with a true love of flying, there shouldn't be much problem with what I call

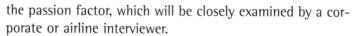

the passion factor, which will be closely examined by a corporate or airline interviewer.

Going back to flying may not be quite so easy for pilots who left the field after turning professional, particularly those who worked for an extended period. These reentry pilots will have to face the close scrutiny of interviewers who will question their passion for and dedication to aviation. The fact that you couldn't feed your family or make your mortgage payments on that meager flight instructor's pay won't appease a chief pilot as he scans your application and asks why you couldn't hack it when the going got rough? What has changed and how are you going to deal with those changes?

Analyzing why you left and why you want to return

To successfully reenter the pilot profession, you'll have to analyze why you left and think long and hard about why you want to return. What has actually changed about both you and the profession since you left it? Is the separation—or shall we call it deprivation—sufficiently life-threatening that you'd be willing to pay the price all over again just to be flying? More importantly, are you willing to back up several steps and enter at a level that may be lower than the one you left?

If you left the cockpit for a desk job after you had tired of instructing and maybe despaired of ever making any upward progress, don't assume that you can return to the field and jump into the right seat of a turboprop without making a few sacrifices. You may well have to go back to that seemingly dead-end CFI job, just to convince a local charter operator that you're serious and worthy of consideration to fly their light twin.

Many pilots forget the importance of having a flying job when they begin their search for a new one. In aviation, this is almost as crucial to success as having the required flight experience. Your ability to endure the worst of times and the lowest pay is an important indicator to your next employer that you're serious about your flying and won't drop out whenever the going gets tough.

Going back to a more prestigious aviation job that does not include actual flying–like sim instruction or a management desk job–will likely raise some eyebrows at interview time. One pilot found that trying to secure that coveted face-to-face encounter without current flight hours required some fancy footwork, due to a seemingly prima donna job choice after leaving the military.

Your job choice and expectations

Your job choice should reflect your passion for flying and demonstrate a willingness to do some drudgery just to be back in the cockpit. If you hold a CFI, that probably equates to giving primary instruction while you're looking for other flying jobs that include more multiengine time.

Talk with friends and relatives, as well as knowledgeable pilots, to acquire a clearer understanding of just how your return to flying may or may not fulfill your expectations. If your plans are based on the idea that everyone else is doing it, why shouldn't you, then be prepared to be disappointed. You'll find that many of the reasons you left are still eliminating pilots and remain the focus for pilot interviewers who want to determine if you're going to be seeking that nonexistent pot of gold.

If you're a person for whom the prospect of *not* flying overrides all the projected sacrifices and downsides, then be prepared for some pointed questions and the need to demonstrate by your actions that you are very serious about your flying and have learned that living without flying is like experiencing the proverbial day without sunshine. You'll likely encounter some "light chop" en route, but accept a sincere "Welcome back," because you're the kind of pilot our profession needs to help all of us enjoy what we honestly believe is the very best job in the world.

Military to Airline: Plan Ahead

Be prepared; plan ahead. As a kid, most of us heard that mantra constantly from our parents and probably didn't give it the attention it deserved. Now, after interviewing several of my coworkers who have military backgrounds, I'm struck by the overwhelming importance of preparation in making a successful transition from military flying to a career with a major airline.

Too often military pilots don't understand just what's involved in making the move, but know they want to—and have to—make the change once their military commitment is complete. To a person, my ex-military contacts agree that the most difficult parts of the process were obtaining accurate data, learning what they had to do to begin the process, and figuring out how to complete each step in a timely manner. Some admitted they didn't have a clue as to what was required for the transition but relied on a squadron "gouge" book, which had some out-of-date and inaccurate material—not a good way to prepare for a lifelong career.

Learning about the differences

Because of the isolation inherent in the armed forces, researching details on an airline career was once quite difficult. Fortunately, with Internet access and the proliferation of websites for various airlines and aviation career services today, finding out about job details and prospective employers is a matter of spending the time to dig for the information. You can learn what's required—how to apply, prepare a resume, and network to secure an interview, as well as how to prepare for and deal with that coveted but stressful event once you have an interview date confirmed.

> The most difficult parts of the process were obtaining accurate data, learning what they had to do to begin the process, and figuring out how to complete each step in a timely manner.

As you prepare to leave the service, recognize that you're about to step into a very different world of aviation. Not only do you face a different type of operation but also the whole focus changes as flying itself becomes the goal rather than just a means to an end. Formerly, your mission, rather than the journey itself, was the focus. Airlines, on the other hand, are concerned with actual flying and at a pace that's unlike anything you have experienced. *How* you get to a destination and *when* you depart and arrive are the basis on which your performance will be judged. Safety comes first, but passenger comfort and adherence to schedule play important parts in the daily routine.

Civilian flying is filled with important details that would have been considered somewhat trivial in the service. Flight attendants, of course, are a new addition, and their job is not only a nice frill but an important safety feature that you'll have to incorporate into your awareness as you strive to fit into the civilian routine. Accommodating another set of priorities can be difficult at times. It is a learned skill—also a necessity, if you expect to survive in your new environment. As I used to phase the dilemma, *never* bite the hand that's going to feed you!

Easing the transition

Before you leave the military, there are several things you can do to ease the transition. Probably most important is to make sure that your last assignment includes some actual stick time, rather than just desk duty, so that your IFR scan is sharp for the sim ride most airlines require. Learn to read Jeppesen charts and study the civilian regulations and procedures, so you are familiar with routine items—like VFR and IFR communications procedures, airspace requirements, and holding speeds. You should be able to discuss these with confidence during an airline interview or demonstrate your knowledge of them during a sim check. (By the way, Jeppesen produces a good transition chart covering the conversion to their format for military users.) In addition, take your written flight engineer exam and analyze your logbooks so you can easily and accurately complete those annoying flight-time grids found on most airline applications.

If you can, do some civilian flying to get a feel for your new aviation environment. Your local aero club is a good and inexpensive place to help ease the transition. Members can explain and demonstrate numerous details that will concern you as you fly to civilian airports, both large and small, controlled and uncontrolled. You're probably used to long runways and a high-dollar support style in your military experience. Now you'll encounter civilian facilities that can range from a full-service FBO, which routinely caters to your every need and likely charges for it, to a small single-runway airport with little more than a pump-your-own fuel pit and an outdoor pay phone to get your weather and ATC clearance. You should become equally at ease with both types.

Other things to consider

In the military, pilots with the highest training scores are assigned the best jobs. Therefore, there's little emphasis on anything other than those high scores. Civilian flying, however, has no such single focus. High scores are great, and at some airlines will determine your seniority number within your new-hire class, but scores will never overshadow the importance of those specific pilot qualities that airline interviewers look for. Your military background doesn't automatically entitle you to pass GO and collect $200. You must demonstrate your leadership skills and ability to follow rules and regulations and make decisions and solve problems, not to mention get along with others in the cockpit—an all-important ability.

Because getting a job is easier when you already have one, my final recommendation is to explore your reserve or guard flying options *before* you separate from the service. You may find that you have to resign your present commission before you can accept one in the reserve to ensure the necessary reserve job priority later. Not having a flying job lined up at separation is tantamount to playing Russian roulette with your career. Don't just assume you'll have no trouble finding a job because of your background; instead make thorough preparations before you leave.

If you've taken all the right steps, your chances of making a smooth transition will be substantially increased. You will have a flying job to help you stay current while you continue your airline job search, and once you've got that new-hire class date, you can continue to fulfill your reserve or guard commitment while you fly the line for your new airline employer.

Chapter 6

LOGS, RESUMES, JOB APPLICATIONS

Logbooks 101:
Neatness Counts

During our interview counseling sessions, we ask our clients to submit a copy of the last three pages of their pilot logbooks and bring their logs with them to a practice interview session. The samples we see range from the sublime to the ridiculous, from the very neat to the incredibly sloppy—and everything in between.

Every log should reflect a pilot's proficiency. Your first logbook is likely a small one, with entries made by your primary flight instructor, as well as yourself, after your first solo. Hopefully, your CFI used tenths of hours, as opposed to minutes, and showed you how to total each column and cross check those numbers before writing the totals in ink.

Your types of pilot time (PIC, Dual Received, SIC) should add up to your total time, as should your day plus night time. Time in different types of equipment flown (SEL, MEL, Glider, Helicopter, etc.) should also add up to your total time. Cross check these totals at the bottom of each page before you transfer them to the next page, to make sure you don't transfer erroneous data.

Completeness and neatness

Ideally, your log should be not only a record of your accomplishments but also a reflection of pride in your fly-

A descriptive log can give a potential employer a good idea of you and your flying habits and provide you with many hours of enjoyment as you review your flying career in years to come.

ing. Notations in the remarks section should describe highlights of your airborne adventures such as "great sunset/sunrise," "first revenue flight," or "gulp, first engine failure!" A descriptive log can give a potential employer a good idea of you and your flying habits and provide you with many hours of enjoyment as you review your flying career in years to come. If the crosswind was blowing at 18 knots or your landing was smooth as glass, say so!

I recommend that you use one color of ink (preferably black) in your log and try to keep it as uniform as possible by using the same type of pen throughout. If you make mistakes, cross-outs and white-out fluid are acceptable, as long as corrections are done neatly. Time logged in error, including simulator in your PIC time, can be deducted with a notation on the next blank line, noting something to the effect that "previous sim time was erroneously logged as PIC, removed from PIC totals as of this date," followed by your signature. This makes the change much easier to follow, whether the reader is an FAA inspector reviewing your log for an ATP written sign-off or an airline interviewer scrutinizing your career to see what airplanes you've flown and how you've logged that time.

Common errors include columns not totaled nor carried forward to the next page; totals completed in pencil, becoming smudged and grimy with age; completed pages not signed; illegible or partial entries with city pairs missing; and large blank gaps left between entries. These blanks might lead someone to think you had plans to fill in the white space but didn't bother or didn't care to do so.

Logbook liabilities

As you get closer to your dream airline job, remember to describe the details of your current job. We see many regional pilots who log their time in a slipshod manner and then expect an airline interviewer to overlook their carelessness. Examples of logbook liabilities include describing a day's flying with a sequence number rather than a description of where you flew; omitting whom you flew with and the types of instrument approaches completed; missing N-numbers; times rounded to the nearest whole number with no tenths showing; missing pages; illogical trip segments and times; and my favorite, a single line for each month's flying—saving paper and showing just how lazy and cheap some pilots can be!

Large white areas in your log can also raise an interviewer's eyebrows. One pilot we worked with preferred to start a new page as he began each new month of flying. There's nothing wrong with this as long as you clearly indicate your system, using lines or arrows to show the completion of that month's flying and signaling the reader to turn the page to find the next month's entries.

Extra points and precautions

Print each entry neatly and do complete the data at the beginning of the log, stating your license history and the period of time covered in this logbook. When presenting your logs for inspection, you can make the reader's job much easier by securing your volumes with a rubber band and placing a neatly lettered sticky note on the outside of each log, stating your name, the volume number, and the beginning/ending dates covered—for example John Jones, Volume 2 of 4, September 1991–July 1995. Tabbing significant events in your aviation career will also help the reader to verify your flying milestones. Taking these simple steps will amaze and impress any interviewer—before you've even had a chance to open your mouth. You might as well score

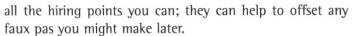

all the hiring points you can; they can help to offset any faux pas you might make later.

A word of precaution—in case you should lose your log-book(s) through fire, theft, or other disaster—every 4 to 6 months copy the last few pages of your current log and store the pages in a secure, fireproof location. Take it from those who've been there, trying to reconstruct a pilot log-book is even harder than trying to bring a stale one up to date—especially before next week's airline interview!

You should be very concerned with the appearance of your logbooks; they are legal documents that reflect your attitude toward flying and show how you regard your avia-tion career. To a potential employer, a logbook can be a good indicator of how you will handle your pilot duties and what kind of an employee you'll be if they choose to hire you. In short, the logbook is a written sample of your behavior. Make sure it's a neat, accurate, and logical description of your hours aloft.

Logbooks:
An Interviewer's Perspective

Our interview counseling sessions are designed to help clients prepare themselves, as well as their paperwork, for close scrutiny by a potential airline employer. We routinely ask to see not only copies of a pilot's employment application, licenses, and FAA medical certificate, but also photocopies of the last 3 pages of his logbooks. An important part of the face-to-face session will be a review of his flying history as seen through the pages of his various logbooks, beginning with that very first, sometimes smudged, often-tattered volume that marked the start of his flying career.

Most pilots are embarrassed by the condition of their first logbook. In an attempt to simulate what they'll likely find at their next airline interview, we tell them to disregard that sentiment and own up to what's in there. You should spend some time reviewing your history, no matter how messy it may seem to you, so you're familiar with your flight experiences and can recall dates and places that pertain to your significant aviation milestones.

Just as an interviewer will pay close attention to each part of pilots' paperwork, so will we carefully peruse their logbooks. We can form a mental picture of people by reading what they've written (or in some cases, *not* written) about the career they claim to be their passion.

What we've seen runs the gamut from delightful to disastrous, from conscientious to compulsive. Because your logbook is a personal record of your flying accomplishments, I'd like to offer some insights on what others will be thinking as they read your entries. More importantly, I'll discuss what you can do to help create a favorable image in their minds, even before they meet you in person.

What interviewers look for

Let's begin by considering what an interviewer looks for when reviewing your logs—often without your being present to explain the entries. Neatness and accuracy are first considerations. Using these samples of your previous work, they'll form an opinion about how well you will complete the flight-related paperwork required of pilots for their airline.

Just as good first impressions in person are important, so logbooks make a strong first statement about their owners.

> **Make your logbook a personal living document rather than a sterile list of flights, dates, and hours aloft.**

Interviewers also look for passion, excitement, and appreciation. Do your comments convey something about you and your motivations? Flight Instructors use the comments block for nuts and bolts information about your flight—such as you performed this maneuver and flew that approach. Pilots who write nothing in the comments section make me wonder if they have any real interest in the profession. Take the time to write something as simple as "great sunset" or "crunch landing" or "first flight for Joe's daughter." You'll enjoy rereading these journal entries later and add to your credibility as a true aviator.

Think about each flight to see if there's something unique that you'll want to remember later. Then, take the time to write your comments and speak your mind in a simple, direct manner that shows your passion for flying. Make your logbook a personal living document rather than a sterile list of flights, dates, and hours aloft.

Correcting errors

Our most frequently asked question concerns how to deal with logbook errors. Corrections—making neat cross-outs or using white-out cover-up fluid to hide offending entries—are certainly permissible. There's no ironclad rule as to which is best. The choice is yours, but if you find the results messy or hard to decipher, take an extra line to explain what corrections you made and why. Then, sign and date that line, attesting to its accuracy.

If your handwriting is poor, print your entries and write them in ink—*never* pencil. What's wrong with pencil? Over time, it will smudge, fade, and look sloppy, whereas ink tends to remain clear and easy to read. Also, the impermanence of pencil may lead the reader to wonder if the author had plans for a few less-than-honorable future entries.

Everything should add up

You can be sure that an interviewer will look to see if your application and resume cross-check correctly with your logbooks. Do the flying jobs you list show up as flight hours during the same time frame? Are the aircraft types the same ones you claim to have flown in your job descriptions? How did you log that right seat time? Are your PIC entries legal and correct for the type of operation and equipment flown?

Speaking of PIC entries, let's cover a much-misunderstood subject: logging of PIC time versus what many airlines count as PIC time. As the author, you are allowed to log flight time any way you like. Just be aware that you'll have to explain it to someone sooner or later. Some airlines feel that pilots who are receiving instruction are not legitimately acting as the Pilot in Command. They feel that the instructor is really in charge of the airplane, even though FARs permit the student to log PIC time (along with the

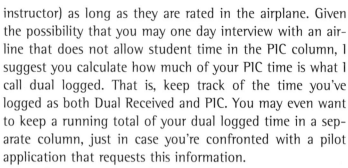

instructor) as long as they are rated in the airplane. Given the possibility that you may one day interview with an airline that does not allow student time in the PIC column, I suggest you calculate how much of your PIC time is what I call dual logged. That is, keep track of the time you've logged as both Dual Received and PIC. You may even want to keep a running total of your dual logged time in a separate column, just in case you're confronted with a pilot application that requests this information.

By the way, prior to the FAA's changing of the rules to allow dual logging of PIC time, there was another easy way to check your total flight time. Just as your types of flight time (SEL, SES, MEL, and MES) should add up to your total time, so you could cross-check your totals by adding your PIC plus SIC plus Dual Received to arrive at your total time as well. Now, with the ability to log PIC time under two different sets of flight conditions, one has to subtract the dual-logged time to make these totals add up correctly.

Dealing with entry gaps

Gaps in your flight entries can not only raise eyebrows but cause you angst as well. How will you account for them during an interview? How will you explain a small amount of flying in days or hours that isn't shown on your other paperwork? You can see why being very familiar with your logs and having the answers to likely questions can help you maintain your confidence in what can be an offensive probe by a wary chief pilot.

One client we counseled was concerned about failing to successfully complete a checkout as a first officer at a small commuter airline flying Beech 99s. His logbook showed several hours of airline instruction, but he left the program shortly thereafter. He was rightly concerned about the entries and knew that just hoping they wouldn't notice them was not a good plan and certainly no way to confront the failure. We discussed the issue from various angles and determined that he was glad to have had the opportunity, but it had come at a time in his flying career when he was ill-prepared to deal with the greater complexity of a turboprop aircraft. Sure enough, about six weeks later when he began his interview with a large regional airline, the first thing the interviewer said was, "Tell us about the two hours of Beech 99 time in your log on 11/15/95." Knowing exactly how to handle the matter, he confronted the issue head-on and was able to discuss it from a position of strength and knowledge.

Doing your own checking

We've covered some questions that can arise as an interviewer checks your logs. Now, let's see how you can reduce stress by performing your own logbook audit. Start by asking another pilot who is not familiar with your flying to look over your logs and note what entries seem unclear or illogical. Have this person total random pages to see if your aircraft categories (SE, ME, etc.) add up to your total time, that your day plus night times equal your total time, and your simulator times are not a part of your total flight hours.

What's day time? Well, just as all logbooks have columns for night flight time, so some (and many more should, in my opinion) have columns for day flight time. It's an easy way to determine total flight time because day plus night equals total flight hours. If you don't have a day column, why not start one? It will make your future calculations and cross-checks much quicker and easier.

Pilots who fly many legs per day may have trouble logging their flight time in a readable fashion. If this is your case, using one line per day of flying is acceptable, as long as you make it clear what and where you flew. Some commuter pilots like to list only a flight pattern number like WE5331. That may make perfect sense to them, but no one else reading it will understand the entry. Instead, spell out what you've done with a notation that explains your routing, even if it means writing out "LAX-SAN-LAX-OXR-LAX-

BFL-LAX-FAT-LAX" at least the first time you fly it. Later, when you repeat the pattern, a simple notation like "Sequence #5331, see above" will now clarify your routing for both you and an airline interviewer perusing your logs.

Shortcuts won't cut it.

You may be tired of logging many entries each month, but don't slip into the habit of listing only your scheduled flying line for the month and figuring you'll back it up with your pay sheets or detailed flying records. A logbook with a one-line-per-month entry will turn off any interviewer. Nor should you plan to bring to the interview a stack of the little red books used by many airline pilots to record their daily flight times. Trying to use them to substantiate your flight time instead of transferring the information to your permanent logbook will only demonstrate just how lazy you are and what little passion you have for airline flying. We know of one regional pilot who had a major airline job in hand—except for his logbooks. When the interviewers saw the stacks of pay sheets and red mini-logs, they told him to return when he got his data properly recorded.

If your flight times are difficult to decipher, spend some time analyzing your logbook and prepare a mini-spreadsheet, showing a clear total for each type of airplane flown along with any notations about errors you may have found. Take the most recent blank line in your logbook and list your findings to bring your log totals up to date.

If you have found only one or two errors from many years ago, you may prefer to use a separate line for each error and list the correction and refer to its date of origin. Then, return to the original error and note on that line the number of hours logged incorrectly on this date, the new date on which it was corrected, and sign the entry.

By the way, some major airlines interview candidates based on their logbook totals as submitted to them on a computer-scored summary sheet. If the totals are not correctly entered or cannot quickly be substantiated by your logbooks, you'll be shown the door before you ever get to an interview. The lesson here is clear: logbook accuracy is of paramount importance to your flying career; make sure your logs match your stated total flight hours.

What about computer logs?

In closing I'd like to add a few words about computer logbooks. Although they look nice and are certainly a good crosscheck for totals, their sterility makes them a poor choice for presentation during an interview. Military pilots may have good reason to supplement their military logs with a computer summary because their records are rather sterile to begin with; they have often been filled out and annotated by nonflying personnel assigned to perform that duty.

As a civilian pilot, you've got your whole history in your pilot log. Take the time to produce a neat, personalized logbook that reflects those qualities that you feel would be an asset to your new employer. You may think those rows and columns in a computer log look neat, but they lack personality and permanence—because they're easily changed with just a keystroke—and they tell the reader little about your character and your passion for your chosen profession. Computer logs, if you choose to use them, should be a supplement or backup to your hand-written professional pilot log.

Don't undo all the good you've done in your flying career by failing to take the time to present your credentials in a time-tested format that reads like a diary and gives the viewer a real insight into your love of the profession. Allow your logbooks to clearly demonstrate the pride you take in your aeronautical accomplishments and your dedication to a flying career.

A Current Resume:
Your Best Sales Tool

Resumes—I think we've all had a love-hate relationship with them. On the one hand, they are tough to assemble and keep current. On the other, a resume is your sales pitch for a very important product: you. It's important that it be concise, accurate, and intriguing. You want to pique the reader's interest so he or she will look closer and call you to come in for an interview.

So how do you make your resume stand out? Well, let's begin by eliminating any tricks or cute gimmicks. Flashy papers, weird type styles, or gee-whiz packaging will gain you nothing but negative points. (One fluorescent green resume received some years ago by a major airline was noticed immediately and routed straight to the trashcan with the thought, "If this is a sample of this pilot's personality, I'd hate to see how he flies!") Remember, in the very straight world of professional aviation, you're looking to conform to a norm rather than stand out like a sore thumb.

What sort of style?

Your resume should convey the best possible image of you in a minimum number of words. Begin with a good quality paper, 8 1/2" x 11", preferably in cream or off-white, and use a clean typestyle that's easy to read. If you have less to say, you can use a larger type size; with more data, you can use a smaller one in the explanatory sections, leaving the basic categories in larger type.

Keep in mind that there are almost as many resume formats as there are people to write them. Choose one that you feel comfortable with and stick with it.

Keep in mind that there are almost as many resume formats as there are people to write them. Choose one that you feel comfortable with and stick with it. Make its format your recognizable trademark, which you can update as your credentials and flight times change. You can also design your own format, as long as it covers the five important areas: personal statistics, flight credentials/flight times, education, employment history, and special accomplishments.

Brevity is important. Stick with one page—period. Two-page resumes rarely get a second glance. Start with your name and vital statistics at the top and include contact numbers, so the reader doesn't have to search for details on who you are or how to contact you. If you tend to move a lot, use a permanent address (your parents' home or a long-term post office box) where you can be assured of getting your mail. Be sure your phone number is correct and check your answering machine regularly. Forget the cute or trendy recorded greeting. Just give the caller a businesslike announcement stating your name, phone number, and how long they have to leave a message.

How to list the pertinent information

Your certificates and ratings should be listed using their full descriptions. If you're a commercial pilot, I suggest you make a heading entitled FAA Certificates and Ratings and then under that list Commercial Pilot: Airplane Single Engine Land, Airplane Multiengine Land, and so forth. I like to put each certificate or rating on its own line so it stands out, particularly important if you don't have a lot of data to include in this section. Be sure to include any written tests completed; your FAA Medical Certificate (preferably Class 1) and the date of issue; as well as your FCC Radio Telephone Operators Permit (you do have one, don't you?).

Flight times should be designated by whole numbers, not rounded to the nearest 10 or 100 hours, and broken down into Total Time, PIC, SIC (if any), ME, Turboprop, Jet, and IFR (both simulated and actual). I recommend that you *not* include cross country, night, or dual given/received because they do not enhance your professional status.

Your education section should contain your college data with dates attended and degree(s) received (for example, University of California, Santa Barbara, CA 1989-1993, B.S. Marine Biology). If you have no degree, list your high school data and any college time you completed, including dates attended and major field of study. I would not include any flight schools attended unless you feel they will enhance your standing with this particular employer. Most airlines could care less where you obtained your primary ratings, but special education courses may well pique their interest in you.

Employment history should be a listing of jobs you've held during the past ten years, starting with the most recent one. Be sure to include the dates for each employer, your title, and duties, and don't forget to give yourself credit where it's due. For instance, rather than just say CFI, describe the type of students you teach and any ground courses or special studies. This will tell a prospective employer what you think of your current job and how you value your own worth.

Wrapping it up

The last section is your opportunity to shine. List here any awards or accomplishments, including scholarships, special recognition, honors, or opportunities that you've received. You can also include anything unique or interesting about your background that might help someone remember you and your talents.

Although such information is not required, you can list your vital statistics—age, height, weight, citizenship, and marital status—if you so desire. It can be helpful in giving the reader a good picture of the pilot you're trying to sell them. All in all, your goal is to present an enticing preview of a pilot they'd like to hire.

Finally, don't worry about not having all the credentials or flight hours you would like. Do your best with what you have and explain your plans for advancement in a short cover letter. Keep a copy of your current resume with you at all times, neatly folded and stored in an envelope. When you've accumulated an additional 50 to100 hours of flying time or six months have passed, send your prospective employers an updated resume.

Remember, appearances *do* count, so use your resume as an opportunity to impress them with your good qualifications and aviation abilities.

Will Your Resume
Get You an Interview?

Several years ago, while sitting in his chief pilot's office, a pilot friend of mine noticed his boss sorting through a large pile of papers with great dispatch. He tossed every second or third sheet into the wastepaper basket and seemed very happy to be making short order of the stack. Curious, my friend asked him what he was doing. "Grading resumes for neatness," he explained. "With so many to choose from, why bother with the ones that aren't neat and orderly? No doubt their flying resembles their paperwork."

> **At most, you have about 20 seconds to make a good impression and pique the interest of your reader.**

In just a few words he had summed up the real crux of a resume: it's a reflection of you and your work habits. It should show you in the very best possible light. Although I could go on for pages about what not to include, here I want to concentrate on how to present your best attributes clearly and concisely. From the story above, you've no doubt deduced that the visual impact of a resume is crucial.

Give them your best.

At most, you have about 20 seconds to make a good impression and pique the interest of your reader. Do it with a good quality white or beige paper—nothing flashy or gaudy. And be sure it's typeset or printed on a high-quality inkjet or laser printer—no dot-matrix printers or ancient typewriters, please.

Regarding the contents, you'll want to show off the best of what you have. It should be a snapshot of your finest applicable attributes—not an autobiographical treatise. Keep it short and to the point. One page, printed on one side, mailed to the recipient in a 9" x 12" manila envelope will make the best impression. A cover letter, containing a two-line summary of your qualifications, can be included, but keep it short and to the point. I recommend the use of cover letters only if they contain information not mentioned in the resume, such as who recommended you for this position.

As to style, there are 100 different ways to organize and present the information. It may be worth your while to invest in a commercial resume preparation service (you do want the job, don't you?) or purchase a do-it-yourself kit from a reputable firm that specializes in aviation resumes. Because the desired information can differ markedly from the needs of other businesses, one of the worst mistake pilots make is to use the wrong format to present their credentials to a prospective employer.

How to present the information

Be sure the data you provide is current, correct, and complete. You may know what Worldwide is, but it may be Greek to a potential employer unless you include the full company name, type of business (if not obvious from the title), location, dates employed and your position or duties.

Your name, address, and phone number should be prominently displayed at the top of the page, followed by these sections: Job Objective, Certificates and Ratings, Flight Experience, Education, Recent Job Experience, and Personal Data. The information that goes into each category should be carefully worded to present your qualifications

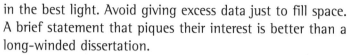

in the best light. Avoid giving excess data just to fill space. A brief statement that piques their interest is better than a long-winded dissertation.

Avoid using jargon, slang, or abbreviations that aren't universal. You're trying to inform the readers, not dazzle them with esoterica. References to cultural, religious, or fraternal organizations should be considered carefully because they might offend the reader and eliminate your resume from consideration.

Finally, before submitting your resume, have an aviation professional critique it to make sure you have not overlooked something important. We have often found items that were omitted by clients because they didn't feel that some of their talents were worth mentioning. On the contrary, special skills can set you apart from other applicants and open the door to that coveted job interview.

Keep your resume current.

While actively job hunting, update your resume when your flight time changes or you add new ratings—at least every six months. Also, keep a clean, neat copy of your current resume with you at all times, with a simple business card attached that contains your name, address, pilot status (Commercial Pilot, CFI with ratings held, ATP or whatever), and phone number. A short run of cards is a small investment, and the cards can be crucial to a successful job search.

Remember, your resume will sell you to a prospective employer. Be sure you present yourself in the best possible light—with a minimum of frills. Let them know you're a professional that they'll be proud to have working for them.

Resume Etiquette

Resumes can make or break your aviation career. Many of our clients come to us with resumes that contain good information but are poorly organized or presented in a sketchy manner. After some editing and several approval drafts, we send them on their way, reminding them that in aviation the messenger can be as important as the message. Said another way: if you have a great message, carefully prepared with clear, concise details of your flying history, don't kill the effect by using inappropriate delivery theatrics that can negate the impact of your presentation.

Major mistakes fall into three general categories: document format (how it looks and what it's printed on), an incorrect delivery method, including both how and to whom the resume is sent, and a grandiose cover letter (a.k.a. foot-in-mouth disease).

The visual impact of your document is crucial. The old saying "You only get one chance to make a first impression" is as true of resumes as it is of meeting someone in person. If the chief pilot or HR person reviewing resumes—and some airlines receive hundreds of them each week—likes the look of yours, he or she is more likely to read your sales pitch. (For specific information about what makes a good first impression, refer to the two articles preceding this one.)

Quantity versus quality

Pilots often complain to us that they've mailed out over 100 resumes with no response. Unfortunately, statistical roulette (read: quantity rather than quality) is rarely the key to a finding a job.

It's better to target your efforts at airlines whose qualifications you meet—or will soon meet at your present rate of building flight time. If you know someone at a particular airline, that's even better. In this case, you should include a cover letter naming the person at the airline who recommended that you apply.

Delivery methods

The method of delivery has been known to annoy and/or offend recruiters before they ever look at the contents. I recently had some eye-opening input from a regional chief pilot concerning unsolicited resumes he had received. His biggest beef was the lack of a correct, current address. It was obvious to him that pilots who really wanted to work for his airline would not mail a resume to the Director of Operations who had retired several years ago. Nor would they use an address that was 24 months out of date and located in another state.

Sending something to the wrong address brands you as inattentive to detail and too lazy to do things right. Chances are it's going to be a hassle for the recipient to send it on to the correct location, if he even bothers. Most airlines today have a website, job hotline, or hiring-information telephone number. You can refer to it or a current industry newsletter to obtain all the correct information about your prospective target before you shoot them a resume—and possibly shoot yourself in the foot!

As to the exact method of delivery, follow the airline's instructions to the letter. If they ask for resumes by facsimile, be sure the machine you use produces a legible copy. Do they want it uploaded to their website? Follow their instructions precisely regarding format, fonts, and page setup. If you're mailing it, be sure to use enough postage and include in your envelope only the items they requested. If a resume only is requested, send just that. If they want copies of your licenses and medical certificate, make sure these are legible, complete (both sides are important), and reproduced in a professional manner.

What about cover letters?

Our first and third major mistakes—the bad resume format and the grandiose cover letter—are closely intertwined. Some pilots never include cover letters, which is OK as long as their resume looks good right out of the envelope. For you cover letter devotees, you must make both documents look good and concentrate on keeping your introductory remarks pertinent, timely, and brief.

Most cover letters are a waste of the readers' time. Thus, one quick glance is about all that a cover letter receives. If you must include one, it should be short and alert them to some important point that may not be readily apparent in the resume. Maybe you're finishing up a course of instruction or have added substantial flight time and/or ratings since you sent your last resume and want to advise them of this fact. Such a cover letter has some meaning and value, and it's important to include it to clarify your enclosures.

Resumes are crucial tools in the pilot's job search. Make sure yours is a current, good quality document that interests the reader from start to finish. Make the best possible impression now, and soon you'll be answering calls to schedule interviews with several employers of your choosing.

Job Applications

Paperwork, paperwork—it seems to be a never-ending chore in our daily lives. But when it comes to job hunting, your "paper-pushing" skills can help you advance in a timely manner if you pay close attention to detail.

When clients come to us for career counseling, our first request is to have them complete our paperwork, just as they would complete documents for a job application. From what we receive, it's obvious many pilots forget that a first impression is usually based on their paperwork. This is their opportunity to dazzle a prospective employer and pique their interest in them and their skills.

Some employers work strictly off of resumes, while others go straight to a standard or customized employment application. Using applications provides them with a level playing field against which to judge all applicants.

You can take advantage of this starting line by making your application neat, concise, and easy to read. First impressions ARE important! As soon as you receive the application, make two copies of each page that requires information. Now, you can work on your copies and fill in all your statistics in pencil, making changes as necessary.

Follow instructions exactly.

Begin by reading the instructions carefully and highlighting any important points. This application may well be a test in itself. Can you follow instructions? If it says to enclose copies of your licenses and medical certificate, be sure to do just that. Too many times, we find that applicants haven't paid close attention to details that are considered very important. "Hmm," muses the personnel specialist, "no attention to detail; did not follow instructions. Is this an indication of how this person will handle a job with us?"

Unless you find instructions to the contrary, complete the application with a good quality typewriter. If necessary, go to a local copy or print shop and use an electronic typewriter with a carbon ribbon, working off the rough draft you've completed earlier. (Both the rough draft and final copy should be proofread by someone other than yourself—preferably another pilot. You want to give yourself every possible advantage.)

If an airline requires you to complete your application in ink or if you don't have access to a typewriter, take your time and make sure your penmanship is neat and legible. Use a black, fine-point pen that will allow you to include all details in a small block.

As you work on your rough draft, be sure to complete each block, or mark N/A if a particular question does not apply to you. Try to give the reader a complete picture of your situation by including all pertinent information. If you've received special awards in school or the community, be sure to include that information, noting dates and locations.

Don't abbreviate anything except the most obvious items. You may know what CVHS means but the reader may have no idea who or what that is and may be annoyed.

When you get to the job history section, be sure to include all the requested details. This means filling in your supervisor's name and phone number—even if your parting was less than pleasant—as well as the last known address of that company. Reasons for leaving—such as better job, pay raise, company ceased operations, position eliminated—should be short and to the point; state them clearly.

Normally, jobs are listed in chronological order with the most recent one first. Many employers ask that you list all previous employment for a specific number of years and explain any periods of unemployment. If you need more space, use a blank sheet and format it to mimic the employment section on the application. If they ask for only 5 years of job history, don't give them 10, figuring more is better. This is a test to see if you can follow instructions.

Most pilot applications have a flight time section or grid. List your flight times in whole numbers—no tenths, please—and be sure your columns and rows are totaled correctly. Also, describe the aircraft types with proper designations such as PA28, BE55, C172, or whatever.

Have your application reviewed.

When you finish your draft copy, have someone who knows you, as well as someone who doesn't, review it. Find out if you've omitted anything important or included something confusing or misleading. You want your application to show you in the best possible light and raise no concerns about your qualifications.

When your application is finally ready to mail, have a friend review it one last time for completeness, all enclosures required, and sufficient postage. If you're in a hurry or want to impress a prospective employer, you can send your application package by air express. However, don't make the mistake of choosing a competing firm if you're applying to a company that's in the shipping business. Mailing your application to UPS via Federal Express is uncool!

Remember, no application is a snap—all require a lot of time and work. But then, if the job is worth it, your close attention to detail can pay you big rewards.

Job Applications: Dos and Don'ts

When airline hiring picks up, we see more and more completed job applications that should never have left the sender's desktop. In their rush to submit their credentials to a potential employer, many pilots forget how important it is not only to present their sterling qualifications but also to demonstrate their ability to follow instructions, express themselves clearly and succinctly in writing, and show the proper concern and respect for the job in question.

Your request for a job application itself should include a short cover letter, stating your basic qualifications, asking for the application, and noting that you've enclosed a self-addressed, stamped envelope (SASE) for their convenience. You may want to include a copy of your current resume, but remember that it might hit the circular file if that company hires only from their own employment applications.

On-the-spot job applications

Some companies interview solely from resumes and request that you complete a job application when you arrive for the interview. In this case, you have to be prepared to complete the paperwork from memory—which is often a test of your logistical planning, attention to detail, and ability to write or print clearly. To limit the panic factor associated with filling out an application on the spot, carry with you a list of your former employers, including names, addresses, and phone numbers as well as dates worked, job title, pay, and reason for leaving. You should also have similar records of your educational background, including special schools or courses attended and any honors or awards received. Now you're ready for anyone's paperwork and can give them complete details without hesitation. You've just passed Part One of their Pilot Employment Test!

Some of the dos and don'ts

Regardless of what system a company uses, make sure your application is filled out completely, using the most current data available. (See the previous article for more details about filling out an application.)

> Regardless of what system a company uses, make sure your application is filled out completely, using the most current data available.

The flight time analysis, or grid sheet, common to many pilot applications can drive you crazy. The format will rarely match your logbook and can take hours to complete. You can lessen the annoyance factor that tends to lead to sloppy, inaccurate work if you do some advance preparation in this area and keep the numbers handy.

Learn the correct designations for the aircraft you have flown and when asked for types, be specific. When asked for aircraft type, using just the manufacturer's name alone (e.g. Cessna) doesn't give the reader enough information, and twin Cessna is even more ambiguous. C-182 or C-421 tells the reader what you've been flying and will save you a lot of probing questions by a human resources interviewer who is trained to determine the accuracy of every block on your application before asking you to proceed to the next stage of the interview. And make sure your times add up correctly—as should each page of your logbook (See previous articles on logbooks for more information.)

In case a recruiter should call you for an interview, your answering machine should have an announcement that is professional (no theatrics or cutesy greetings); you can inform the caller what number they've reached if you prefer not to state your name. More than one job opportunity has been lost as a result of a recruiter being turned off after hearing a childish or inappropriate recording that gave them second thoughts about the applicant. Don't kill the goose before it's had a chance to lay that golden egg.

Recheck your information carefully.

When you're satisfied with your rough draft, ask a pilot friend to proofread it for you, give you an honest evaluation, and note any items that might raise an eyebrow. Then set the application aside for a few days and return to it for the final draft, which should be typed using a good carbon ribbon or printed neatly with black ink.

If you use a professional typist, be sure to double check his or her work. Anyone who is unfamiliar with aviation data and terminology can make mistakes. Finally, take your finished product to a nonpilot friend and ask that person to proof the document for spelling, syntax, and grammatical errors.

If you need to attach an extra sheet to complete your job history, be sure it is organized using the same column headings as the corresponding section on the application. Your goal is to impress the employer with this preview of you, their next new-hire pilot.

If you're mailing your masterpiece and are concerned about its delivery, you can include a self-addressed stamped postcard to be completed simply with a date-received notation. Now sit back, relax, and enjoy a rest. Completing job applications properly is demanding work and, hopefully, your flying career will reward you accordingly.

Job Applications:
What Companies Want

If you've done any interviewing lately, you've no doubt noticed the attention given your employment application by the Human Resources (HR) Department. From the smallest detail of your flight hours to a recitation of each job you've ever held, they want to know it all—and in 3-part harmony! So what's the big deal? Why are they such sticklers for details? Who cares about or even knows the phone number of your long-bankrupt charter employer from 10 years ago?

During our interview and career-counseling sessions, we review applications submitted by our clients and try to give them some idea of what a company looks for when they receive an applicant's paperwork. The first and most obvious concern is the visual impact of your application. If you have previously sent them a resume, that document was your opportunity to impress them with your individuality and special qualifications. Now, as you present your completed application, you're being directly compared to your competition—same form, same requested information—a level playing field, so to speak.

It's part of the job.

Because paperwork and attention to detail are so much a part of the professional pilot's job, this is your first chance to impress an employer with your ability to fit right in where it counts. Neatness and following instructions to the letter are going to net you points and predispose recruiters to viewing the contents favorably. You want to show them immediately that you possess a number of the qualities they seek, including paying attention to detail, neatness, thoroughness, patience, and the ability to read and write clear, concise English with no misspellings.

Let's spend a moment on that phrase "attention to detail." Perhaps the most frustrating part of reading an application is dealing with missing or incomplete information. When you leave something blank, it sends the message that you either forgot to complete that item or didn't proofread your work. It's amazing how much you can convey through your omissions! A simple N/A would have left the reader with a more favorable impression.

Incomplete items are another annoyance. We typically see these in the education section, where a pilot just assumes the reader will not linger. But education IS important to an employer, and even if your credentials are a bit on the skimpy side, be proud of what you've accomplished and state clearly "high school diploma" (even if it sounds repetitive to you) in the box that says "Degree." Describe all formal education you've received, and if it was obtained outside the United States under a different educational system, add a separate sheet and note how the grade levels there compare to those of an American high school or university.

Is your information detailed and clearly stated?

Clarity is even more important as we consider job descriptions. "Pilot, Part 135 airline" doesn't give the reader any information about your actual job or flight duties. However, "First Officer and Captain on DHC-6 flying scheduled passenger operations in Southern California" provides a complete picture of your job, the environment, and the equipment you flew.

Remember, the more details you provide now, the fewer questions you'll have to answer later. It might help you be specific to imagine the reader is from a foreign country and can't pass your paperwork on for interview scheduling until he understands every item you've included. Don't try to impress him with meaningless verbiage. Instead, provide complete and honest answers to the questions that will convey a clear picture of your employment history and experience.

Don't understate or underrate your qualifications. Reticence can cause a recruiter to question your interest in the job or your assertiveness and ability to sell yourself. Show the pride you take in your work by giving yourself credit for your own accomplishments. (One common error we see is describing CFI qualifications using grocery-store terminology. Please, use certificated flight instructor—not certified which is used by government meat inspectors and public accountants.)

Remember that a job application can be much more than a dry rendition of your vital statistics. Spend some time on those job descriptions and make sure they sell your skills to this prospective buyer. Explain any ancillary job duties. Some small detail may be just the quality that will set you apart from other applicants and give you the chance to enrapture the interviewer with your knowledge of antique aircraft parts or volunteer work with the local air scouts.

When you're offered the chance to "tell us anything else you think we should know about you," don't waste this valuable opportunity by leaving it blank. Everyone has something that makes him or her unique. This is a test to see if you'll seize the opportunity to sell yourself! Mediocrity is *not* rewarded, but talented, interesting individuals frequently are—with an interview slot to see if they're as impressive in person as they are on paper.

Scrutinizing Your Own Airline Application

There seems to be no middle ground when it comes to completing airline-pilot application forms. Pilots universally love the results (getting interviewed and ultimately hired) and hate the nightmare process of reworking an application to get it right.

Your natural inclination may be to hurry up and get the completed application in the mail. But submitting paperwork that doesn't show you at your best is a form of professional suicide and akin to careless and reckless flight operations. Small mistakes in your paperwork will probably net you large frowns, as will overly gushing narratives or inappropriate language. Think carefully about those seemingly standard questions before you answer them and, as you would do with an interview question, ask yourself, "Why did they ask me this question?" Better yet, consider what your answer or the way you've presented the information will tell them about you.

Your goal is to provide a clear, concise picture of your background, skills, and accomplishments in a format they, not you, have chosen. Fill in all their squares and check all their boxes. Provide the information they request but don't feel you have to display every blemish and flaw. Rather, answer questions to your advantage, leaving an opportuni-

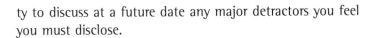

ty to discuss at a future date any major detractors you feel you must disclose.

Get it right the first time.

To begin with, save yourself time and frustration by making copies of the blank application and complete your first (or second or third) draft on the copy. You'll probably go through several rewrites before you reach a final version that can be retyped on the original form, but it's certainly worth the trouble to get it right on your initial submission.

Sending corrections—other than updates showing increased pilot experience—that substantially change your vital statistics or essay information can leave interviewers wondering about your professional pride and attention to detail. Furthermore, they may become concerned about the underlying reasons for these changes when they compare your most recent submission with your previous application(s). This is not to say you can't change an application when pertinent new information becomes available. Just be careful not to send trivial changes in an attempt to raise your profile.

Wrestling with mini-essays

Certain mini-essay questions can stump pilots, causing them to submit trite, meaningless gobbledygook that leaves the reader wondering about their fluency with the English language. Questions about your most and least favorite previous jobs, as well as the catch-all, "anything else we should know about you," are opportunities to show your maturity and passion for aviation.

Use the question about your worst job to clearly and briefly state your feelings about a position that didn't contain those aspects you eagerly anticipate in this new one. If your job flipping burgers was routine and wasn't flying, say so. For your best-job answer, describe one that did offer some great flying or provided experience at challenging airports or perhaps included multiple duties that allowed you to use more than just your flying skills. Any essay question should be carefully worded and edited for brevity and sincerity. Saying something that could be viewed as conceited or self-righteous will lessen the overall impact and might cause in-depth questioning at a subsequent interview.

When are you available for work?

Eager pilots want to state that they can start a job immediately, but what does that say about the responsibility they feel toward their present employer? Remember, leaving an employer without proper notice will likely show up in a background check. "Two weeks notice" is an appropriate response that shows compliance with standard business etiquette. This will also allow your current employer to respond in the affirmative if asked during a routine background check "Is this applicant eligible for rehire?" Said another way, did you follow all the proper steps for an impending job change?

Employment record: condensed version

The employment-record section seems to be another difficult area for applicants to complete satisfactorily. Used properly, it can reveal what job you actually did and how you felt about it. But you're probably wondering how to convey so much information in a condensed area, which is often no more that two inches wide and three or four lines long. In a word: show your enthusiasm.

The column for "Job Title and Duties" can give your reader some insight into your character, depending on what you say and how you phrase it. With careful wording, you can convey real interest (or disinterest) as well as pride (or disdain) for your current or past employment. Think about the difference between a curt "CFI" in this section versus "CFI and Assistant Chief Flight Instructor, designing and teaching accelerated flight/ground courses." In the second case, just a few descriptive words conveyed a positive attitude that would impress an employer with the applicant's real passion and desire to excel.

Moving on to the "Reason for Leaving" column brings us to another common error. Time and again we see excessive use of the catch-all phrase "career advancement." To a future employer, it can indicate anything from you're being afraid to state the real reason you left to you're too lazy, indifferent, or even ignorant to give the precise information that would tell them something about you, your job aspirations, and your career progression.

If the company you worked for ceased operations, that's easily stated. (By the way, if this is the case, provide the personnel information that was true at the time you worked there. You may also want to supply an independent source who can verify your employment during that period.) If you left your employer because you were concerned about downsizing and getting furloughed, that's a reasonable concern. If safety was a concern and the equipment was marginal, that's also a legitimate reason for leaving.

If the opportunity to fly bigger, faster, more sophisticated equipment was the reason you left, then say so! You would be surprised at how many subtle points you can gain with a description that shows your passion for flying. Avoiding a bland, non-descriptive answer is important.

However, don't give yourself an unnecessary bad rap as did one client who wrote "terminated," in the reason-for-leaving box. His position at a major airline was eliminated when the company sold the DC-10s on which he had been a flight engineer. Saying "terminated," rather than "job category eliminated," could give any reviewer a good reason to trash his application and assume the worst.

What to do about "gray areas"

Is an application the place to disclose any skeletons? It depends. You might do yourself more harm than good by saying too much when a question actually asks very little.

One pilot we know went into an excessive discussion about missing a scheduled airline trip because he misread his show time and ended up 2.5 hours late for work.

His answer gave too many details for a simple question that asked "How many times have you been late or absent for work in the past 12 months and how much time did this absence represent?" A simple "1 time" and "1 day" would have sufficed, leaving a detailed discussion for the job interview. Later, when facing the recruiter, the pilot could have used this event to answer a question about a time he had done something he regretted later.

Other skeleton-type questions can often be handled by knowing enough about the situation to determine if the event is one that actually requires reporting. The traffic violation section of your application may seem to be the place to bare your soul about an incident that appears on your record, but check with the DMV first. In one case we know of, the event did not warrant a write up because it was not a violation, even though it was listed on the applicant's driving record. Again, it was something that could be used to answer one of those general HR questions or that catch-all "anything else you would like us to know about you" question.

If you are applying to an affiliated airline that has access to your current employer's files, realize that the affiliate will gain a greater depth of knowledge about you than an independent airline will. Said another way, if the missed-trip event discussed above was at issue in a flow-through or right-of-hire situation, then you can be sure that everything in your personnel file will be available for scrutiny and proceed accordingly.

Used properly, a seemingly bad situation can be turned into a discussion that might net you some points for disclosing something that shows a character asset you possess. That you want to share this knowledge demonstrates your honesty and openness about your past. If you have such a glitch in your background, consider it carefully and consult a knowl-

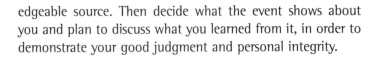

edgeable source. Then decide what the event shows about you and plan to discuss what you learned from it, in order to demonstrate your good judgment and personal integrity.

Gaps in your records

Be careful about gaps in your employment and flying records. They will be checked. One pilot we assisted asked us if he thought his failing in a new-hire ground school at a small commuter airline would kill his chances of being hired by another company. His logbook showed 5 hours of 19-seat turboprop time and then nothing for the next six months while he went job hunting.

We told him to be honest about his failure and admit he had received a chance at a regional pilot slot before he had gained enough experience to handle the sophisticated equipment. This gave him a good reason to discuss what he had learned from the event and the fact that he was very glad to have had the opportunity to try, even though it did not work out at the time.

As it turned out, his interview session began with "tell us about that turboprop time in your logbook"—precisely the area he'd been concerned about discussing. Having prepared for just such a query, he was now ready with an honest, non-defensive reply that dealt directly with the issue. It was exactly the information they were looking for, and he was subsequently hired by his first-choice major airline.

Job applications are important documents. (Be sure you keep a copy of your final version—the one that's neatly typed.) You may send the resume with a short cover letter but, remember, what's important is how you fill out the paperwork. As a company scrutinizes your application now, it will gain some idea of how you will survive in their pilot environment later. Be concise, be honest, and be descriptive. With some careful rewrites you can convey your unique qualifications and dedication to flying, along with your enthusiasm for their airline.

Chapter 7

INTERVIEW BASICS

Interview Preparation: A Multistep Process

Preparing well for an upcoming interview can be one of the most important factors in determining whether or not you get the job. There are many things you can do to enhance your chances of success, even before you get the call or letter to schedule an interview date.

Begin your preparation several months ahead by becoming informed about the industry in general and your target company in particular. If you don't subscribe to an aviation publication such as *Aviation Week & Space Technology, Air Transport World, Business and Commercial Aviation,* or *Professional Pilot,* find someone who does and ask him to save you old issues. You can also pull up on-line aviation newsletters and websites and scan for articles that pertain to current events in your area of aviation—such as corporate, regional, or major airline. Try to expand your horizons by reading about topics beyond your present professional level. Know what's happening in the world you wish to enter, particularly as it pertains to your target employer. You may be asked to discuss industry changes in an interview.

Researching the target

Keep a file of articles on your target airline(s) and seek out their pilots and public-contact employees whenever possible to gain insight into company workings. Start net-working. Ideally, you should talk to someone who has been interviewed recently and can give you current information. Senior employees are good sources of inside information but are rarely familiar with recent interview practices (unless they actively participate in the process). So, ask employees you meet if they know of anyone who's been hired within the last six months who might be willing to talk with you.

If you don't know anyone at your target airline, join an on-line aviation forum and ask detailed questions to deter-mine what type of pilots are getting interviews, who's being hired, how long it's taking from interview to class date, and what are their future hiring and equipment expansion plans. You can gather extensive insider's information just by asking politely. Try to converse with people who have the job you seek. Remember, however, that talk is just that. Don't ask a correspondent for any favors, such as putting in a recom-mendation or a good word for you. This will put the employ-ee in an awkward position and could boomerang later.

Check your local library or on-line news service for such additional information as new routes, airplane acquisitions, and company news. Also, follow the company's stock prices so you'll know what's happening to their financial situation in particular and the airline industry in general. If the com-pany is a public corporation, call your local stock broker and request a copy of the annual report. Obtain a copy of the airline's in-flight magazine as well and pay particular atten-tion to their route map showing cities served and any code-sharing or alliances with other airlines. Save advertisements from national or regional publications. Your files will be brimming with information before you know it!

Preparing yourself

Now that you've researched an airline's history, it's time to work on yours. Be sure your resume is current and con-cise and a maximum of one page. Gather your records, including driving, credit, and educational, and make sure they are correct and speak well of you. If not, be prepared to explain the circumstances surrounding any questionable event. If you're not sure how to handle a tricky situation, like an FAA violation or employment termination, get some professional advice to make sure you handle a potential minefield with care and confidence.

Gather your letters of recommendation and make sure they're current and pertain to the interview situation at hand. Producing a former letter of recommendation that describes your virtues for another purpose—perhaps a scholarship application—will only confuse the interviewer and make that person wonder why you provided backup that's not applicable to the task at hand. (It's kind of like planning a cross-country flight with outdated weather information.)

Get to work on your reading list. Begin with a good general text on interviewing such as H. Anthony Medley's *Sweaty Palms* or *Interview for Success* by Ron and Caryl Krannich. Also read airline-specific titles such as Irv Jasinski's *Airline Pilot Interviews*, Norris and Mortenson's *Airline Pilot Career and Interview Manual*, and Cheryl Cage's *Checklist for Success*. Each of these books has a good list of questions you'll be expected to answer, so begin to compile your own responses that detail your personal, professional, and education accomplishments.

More subjects to study

Once you're familiar with interview techniques, move on to the psychological testing section. Many airlines administer these tests, and the more familiar you are with them, the better. Most bookstores carry a generic text by ACCO entitled *Officer Candidate Tests*, and you can order specific books from aviation vendors that contain sample tests airlines are known to use.

The other important area of study is aviation itself. You're expected to demonstrate a knowledge level com-

An ATP prep manual will also give you a good overview of what you're expected to know, and don't forget to sharpen your basic math and vocabulary skills!

mensurate with your flight time. Review the FARs, Parts 61, 91, and 135, the AIM, AFD, Aviation Weather, Jeppesen introductory pages, and your airplane FOM, with special attention to limitations and emergency procedures. An ATP prep manual will also give you a good overview of what you're expected to know, and don't forget to sharpen your basic math and vocabulary skills!

Whew—this seems like a lot of material to cover! It is, indeed, and you can see why it's important to start early and be thorough in your preparation. If you would like help with your brush-up program, consider getting some professional interview counseling to polish your presentation and help you deal with any rough spots that may lurk in your background. Such preparation can be especially helpful if you have any sticky situations to discuss or have had several unsuccessful interviews in the past.

Now is the time to plan for the future and do everything in your power to ensure your success. You wouldn't take a checkride without hours of preparation, would you? So give that upcoming job interview your very best effort. The results will be well worth it.

Interview Attitudes: Are Yours Appropriate?

Ideally, an upcoming interview should be your last, concluding with the job offer of your dreams (or if this isn't your dream job, at least the one you want for the foreseeable future). So you're going to act like it's the one place you want to be. Why? Because attitude is probably the biggest plus or obstacle to getting hired anywhere, particularly at an airline where they have applications exceeding pilot slots by the hundreds, and sometimes by the thousands.

We recently assisted two clients with interview counseling for a large regional airline. One of them went in with an enthusiastic, this-is-where-I-want-to-be attitude and later reported to us how professional and personable everyone was and how great it was to get the opportunity to interview with them. The other, feeling that regional flying was a bit beneath him, didn't expend much effort on the process, forgot to turn in his completed paperwork at the interview, and found the atmosphere unfriendly and indifferent.

Who do you think got a job offer? Perhaps the first applicant's attitude had something to do with it? Even though their qualifications were dissimilar (the second applicant actually had many more hours of flight time than the first), what counted most in our service-oriented industry was attitude. Credit for those thousands of flight-time hours was lost when applicant number two was unable to

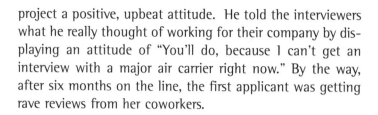

project a positive, upbeat attitude. He told the interviewers what he really thought of working for their company by displaying an attitude of "You'll do, because I can't get an interview with a major air carrier right now." By the way, after six months on the line, the first applicant was getting rave reviews from her coworkers.

Three other factors that count

Attitude is probably the biggest factor to consider, but remember that looks, actions, and words are also important. Let's look at these three factors and how they'll affect your chances of success.

I listed looks first because your initial impression is always what counts most. The classic "You've got 20 seconds to make a good impression" is very true in aviation, where pilots are held in high esteem and expected to set a good example for everyone. Be sure that you're dressed appropriately for the occasion, wearing nothing trendy or flashy. There are numerous manuals that give tips on what to wear for an interview, but normally a conservative suit of the same color as the airline's pilot uniforms will help the interviewer see you in your desired new role.

Wearing the wrong thing can be disastrous; I found this out years ago when an applicant I had recommended to a major airline was given a strange brush-off after the initial interview. Inappropriate dress had been the cause, and the interviewer had felt uncomfortable sending this applicant to the captain's board. Fortunately, I learned about the incident in time to recommend an acceptable solution: a new conservative blue suit!

After attitude and looks, actions and words run a close tie for third place. Because they're so closely intertwined, each should complement the other. You have to act like the mature, professional pilot you're describing in your responses. Your actions will precede your words when you're judged by the office personnel you meet as you arrive for your interview. Be sure you arrive early, well-rested and fed, and prepared for a close scrutiny of your credentials. Remember, you've been approved on paper, now it's time to reinforce that opinion in person.

> After attitude and looks, actions and words run a close tie for third place. Because they're so closely intertwined, each should complement the other.

Be polite to everyone you meet, and expect to do a lot of sitting and waiting around— two sure things in a pilot's career! Bring some professional reading to keep you occupied and try to avoid speculative discussions with other applicants. You're being scrutinized in the waiting room, the cafeteria, the medical offices, the hotel van, even on the flight to the interview.

Greet your interviewers with a smile, firm handshake, and good eye contact. You're glad to be there, and your positive first impression is underway.

Good responses to interview questions

Probably the most important questions you'll be asked at an interview are, "Tell us about yourself" and "Why should we hire you?" Good preparation can go a long way toward making the answers to these two questions sales pitches for your good points that can distinguish you from the competition and leave a favorable impression with your interviewers.

Other questions will probe your technical competence as well as your leadership ability, problem-solving skills, work record, employee relations, and how you deal with conflict situations. There are numerous good interview books available. Find one that has a style you can relate to and read it carefully, paying close attention to how to project your best side as you answer each question.

If you have any problem areas—for example, violations, a bad driving record, or credit problems—in your background, practice answers that delve deeply into the whys and hows

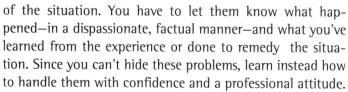

of the situation. You have to let them know what happened—in a dispassionate, factual manner—and what you've learned from the experience or done to remedy the situation. Since you can't hide these problems, learn instead how to handle them with confidence and a professional attitude.

Most important is to understand each question and answer it concisely to your own advantage. Remembering that this interview is a sales pitch for you, be sure to sing your own praises and emphasize the skills you have to offer. There's no need to tell them about your weaknesses. Pitch your strong points and drive home the unique talents that make you well-suited to the job.

Finally, thank the interviewers for the opportunity to meet with them and conclude with your personal summation of why they should hire you. When it's over, send a short thank you note to each person, a reminder of who you are and what you can do for the company. Then sit back and wait. With your good attitude and skillful handling of the interview, you may just get the job!

Why Won't They Interview Me?

"Why won't they interview me?" is probably the universal cry of unemployed pilots everywhere. We've all heard incredible stories about lucky friends and acquaintances with minimal time and experience getting interviewed for a corporate or airline job. What's their secret? Why are they getting interviews and you're still waiting for the phone to ring?

We recently heard a woe-is-me story from a ground instructor for a large flight-training company. Possessing an unblemished military record, he was eagerly trying to break into civilian airline flying with what he considered to be good credentials and superior skills. He had recently completed a pilot interview with a major air carrier and was stunned to be rejected, whereas two of his buddies with similar backgrounds were busily wading through new-hire ground school at the same airline. Moreover, his lack of additional interview invitations led him to believe that no other airline would interview him without a personal inside contact to ease the way.

What can hold you back

On previous pages I've talked about the value of networking to demonstrate your credibility and dedication to your aviation career. What's important here is to note the proper order of events: demonstrate first, network second.

Said another way, don't expect someone to recommend you without having known you and your abilities for some time. You have to build an impressive resume, with credentials appropriate to the position you're seeking, that shows not only what you've done, but also how you've gone about achieving your aviation career goals.

Perhaps a lackluster resume is hampering our instructor who can't get an interview. Maybe the personal recommendation that netted him his last interview was accompanied by some ho-hum paperwork. If so, he may now be pointing a finger at the wrong culprit, believing that who you know will always triumph in the interview game.

> Your credentials—and how you present them—are very important, as are your enthusiasm and interest in your profession and related disciplines.

Because every pilot's background is unique, we can't give appropriate advice without first getting a full history on each individual, but there are certainly a number of red flags that go up each time we hear this type of lament. Your credentials—and how you present them—are extremely important, as are your enthusiasm and interest in your profession and related disciplines.

Airlines, of course, are interested in your education, flight time, and employment history. Your most recent job, however, can be a real eye-opener to both a chief pilot sorting resumes as well as an interviewer screening applicants. Both are looking for some evidence of your dedication to and sacrifices made for your aviation career.

Building quality flight time

Flight instructors often have an edge when it comes to demonstrating their passion for flying. Building flight time is difficult—particularly getting past that wasteland between 400 and 1,000 hours. It takes time, patience, and perseverance, often with low pay and long hours. Airlines realize the sacrifices that CFIs make to achieve their goals.

However, once you've passed the 1,000-hour mark, it's definitely time to start seriously beating the bushes for quality multiengine time. Many airlines consider more than 1,000 hours of single-engine time (whether dual given or PIC) to be worthless and indicative of a real lack of desire to upgrade skills and credentials.

Similarly, *not* obtaining your ATP certificate as soon as you're qualified makes an employer wonder just how serious you are about your airline aspirations.

In the case of our military-pilot-turned-ground instructor, the human resources representative sorting resumes may wonder why this pilot is doing ground training when he should be actively flying and learning the civilian ropes. Perhaps he's not willing to endure the entry-level wages and benefits at a regional airline. Is this type of work beneath the pilot in question? Does he carry with him superiority hang-ups from his previous high-quality flight experience in the military? Does he appear to want all the benefits without paying any of the dues? This *is* a major hurdle that many pilots from both civilian and military backgrounds must overcome to land an interview and secure a job.

Proper preparation is necessary.

We've seen many pilots, tired of the corporate or charter flying they have done comfortably for many years now decide to jump on board the airline bandwagon. They see fellow aviators getting interviews with qualifications similar to their own and talk themselves into the why-not-me mode without carefully analyzing what they have to offer and how to present their credentials in a credible, effective manner. Many times what they consider to be an equal background is actually quite different, requiring a unique and persuasive sales pitch. As we've mentioned before, a good resume, based on excellent qualifications, can be the differ-

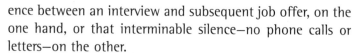

ence between an interview and subsequent job offer, on the one hand, or that interminable silence—no phone calls or letters—on the other.

An employment application requires a lot of time and attention to reflect accurately your best attributes. Interview invitations are a confirmation of your successful salesmanship. You've intrigued them with your good qualifications. Now you have to carry the program to its logical conclusion with a positive, upbeat interview that sells your skills in a persuasive, believable manner.

Don't fall into the habit of complaining about your lack of interview opportunities. Take positive steps to steer your career in the right direction. Do some careful evaluating to see what improvements you can make. Interviews aren't impossible to obtain; careful planning and hard work will prepare you for this much sought-after opportunity.

Avoiding Canned
Interview Responses

It's got to be an interviewer's nightmare—or sleeping pill, depending on your point of view—having to listen to one canned response after another, with none of them giving any clue as to how the pilot applicant really thinks or acts or responds to some common cockpit situations.

We've all been told of the dangers of parroting back to an interviewer whatever you think he or she wants to hear. So why, then, does this practice continue? A few reasons come to mind: ignorance—not knowing what's wanted or required—lack of preparation, laziness, and/or just plain misunderstanding of the whole interview process.

If you give a rote recital that demonstrates nothing about your personal, professional, or educational experience, the interviewer gains no insight into your personality, character, or people skills.

Because pat answers affect the interviewer in such a negative manner, it's important for everyone, especially pilots, to recognize the annoyance, boredom, and frustration induced by a standard, canned answer in response to a question seeking specific information. If you give a rote recital that demonstrates nothing about your personal, professional, or educational experience, the interviewer gains no insight into your personality, character, or people skills. Realizing that canned answers are akin to professional suicide, let's look at a better approach—answering questions with a personal style that gives the interviewer a clear understanding of you and your abilities.

The ideal interview

In the best of all worlds, the pilot interview would involve flying a three-day trip with you, getting to know how you act and react, discussing your views on various subjects. Then, your captain could see exactly how you relate to other crew members and handle leadership and problem-solving situations. In other words, he could assess whether or not you handle the job in a professional manner that's consistent with company policy—and are still a fun and interesting person to fly with.

Since this ideal interview scenario isn't a realistic possibility, you should fashion your responses to give the interviewer an inside look at your real personality. At the same time you must recognize that you're in an interview situation and choose your words carefully, making them genuine, persuasive, and personalized to your own particular situation.

Why do you want to work for our company?

Let's take a look at one of my top nominees for the question that typically gets a canned answer: Why do you want to work for ABC Airline? This query seems to elicit unimaginative, rambling, trite answers from pilots using language that's just not believable. Pilots seriously interested in the profession have to know they will be asked this question and should prepare accordingly.

During a recent interview-preparation session, one of our clients answered this question by listing the company's accomplishments, making his recitation sound more like a sales brochure. He mistakenly thought that spouting the past three years' annual earnings statistics would convince an interviewer of his deep knowledge about the company. Unfortunately, he chose to answer a question he wasn't asked—"What do you know about our company?" And he compounded the damage by his choice of words and phrases, many of which resembled those found in a legal document rather than his own vocabulary.

You're not auditioning for valedictorian of the year, so use good everyday English that demonstrates your sincerity and reflects your unique personality. Use words that sound like you and are believable, given your background and education. You want an interviewer to feel that the emotions you express are sincere and that you can do a professional job in a manner that's a credit to the company. You're not some politician being hired for your ability to recite a prepared speech.

Choose a maximum of three or four items and say them with sincerity and enthusiasm. Your answer might describe your lifelong desire to work for the company since you first rode their airline as a child. Or it might reflect how impressed you've been with their growth and by the enthusiasm of employees you know who really enjoy working there. Something this simple, expressed in your own words with heartfelt sincerity, can earn you many more points than describing the company's far-flung route structure or impressive stock earnings—all of which sound thoroughly unbelievable to an interviewer who has heard every line of patter numerous times.

Why should we hire you?

The criteria described above apply as well to the question, "Why should we hire you?" Remember, this is your chance to sell your most outstanding skills and character traits. You must convince recruiters that you're more than just a good pilot who loves to fly. Describe other skills that will benefit the company. Maybe you love to teach and have experience writing technical manuals. Talk to them about your passion for flying and the joy and satisfaction you derive from going that extra mile, as well as the personal satisfaction you get from helping those around you perform to your same high standards.

Don't compare yourself to other pilots but measure your success against your own yardstick. Relate how you deal with challenges and help those around you improve their work environment as well. Describe the extra efforts you make in your daily routine that demonstrate you're not just another "wannabe" pilot. A healthy dose of sincerity can go a long way toward improving your credibility and demonstrating that you have what it takes to do the job and be an asset to the company.

Selling your real self is the goal of interviewing. Too many pilots figure it's cool to understate their enthusiasm and they try to sound suave and sophisticated. Wrong! You have to prove you're passionate about working for their company and let them feel your kid-in-a-candy-store excitement. In the final analysis, if you can convince interviewers that you're someone who really enjoys the work, gets along well with others, and is proactive in the workplace, you've got an excellent chance of beating the odds and filling that left seat even sooner than you had planned.

Why Won't They Hire Me?

On previous pages I've talked a lot about what you can do to enhance your chances of getting hired at an airline. But after all is said and done, what can you do if you get an awful letter telling you thanks, but no thanks?

Don't think of it as the end but rather as a beginning. Consider this a time for some reflection and analysis and then go back to the drawing board to analyze what might have gone wrong. Perhaps we should rephrase the question from "Why won't they hire me?" to "Why SHOULD they hire me?" in order to come up with some good strategies to deal with the inevitable ego crushing that often results from a rejection letter.

Do I have the right qualifications?

If you made it to an interview, it's probably safe to say you met the company's qualifications and that is not your limiting factor. However, there are always exceptions to this rule, evidenced by one applicant who did an outstanding job during the interview process only to be turned down with the recommendation that he reapply in another year.

This pilot, although well qualified, was rather young and had just started working for a subsidiary company. It was common knowledge that pilots were not eligible for employment at the parent company until they had flown a certain minimum of hours at the affiliate in order to amor-

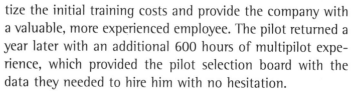

tize the initial training costs and provide the company with a valuable, more experienced employee. The pilot returned a year later with an additional 600 hours of multipilot experience, which provided the pilot selection board with the data they needed to hire him with no hesitation.

So here's a case where a pilot's qualifications were good enough to get him an interview, but not quite good enough to get him hired—a slight variation on our theory that getting the interview means your qualifications are OK. Employers will often interview candidates who have less than their minimum requirements because they come with a strong recommendation from another employee or, perhaps, the pool of available qualified pilots has dwindled substantially. In either case, your job is to convince them that your deficiency is not a limiting factor.

When the competition is stiff

Sometimes you'll find that your superior qualifications and dynamite interview skills let you down for no discernible reason. Now is the time to consider your competition and understand that many companies have the difficult choice of picking the top qualifiers from a field of high-scoring applicants. You may be encouraged to reapply on their next cycle because you would have been hired if only there had been fewer well-qualified applicants to choose from.

Still, you're probably depressed at the outcome and wondering what you could do differently the next time around. Spend a few moments now, while the events are still fresh in your mind, and review your application and interview with a critical eye. What steps might you have taken to improve your chances? You may decide you would like an independent analysis to help point out possible areas for improvement. Combing your application, resume, and logbooks may yield a few details you overlooked that could have tilted the selection committee's decision in your favor.

Reviewing the interview

The big qualifier is, of course, the interview itself. But, try-ing to analyze your own performance can be tough—particu-larly if you're not experienced and think everything went just fine. Sometimes overconfidence or cockiness can be a killer in itself. The proper amount of humbleness can go a long way in demonstrating your respect for the process, along with your genuine enthusiasm for the specific job at hand.

To help ease the disappointment, you may want to write down your honest answers to the following questions: What kind of rapport did I establish with the interviewer(s) and how quickly did this occur? Were my answers succinct and to the point, relating my personal, professional, and educational background to their specific query? Did I look and act like I really wanted the job, as well as showing that I am knowl-edgeable about the workings of their company?

> You have to convince a recruiter that you have the technical knowledge, leadership ability, social interaction skills, and willingness to conform to company policy and procedures that will make you a desirable employee who's a credit to their organization.

This could be a checkride.

I could go on and on about what you, as an applicant, need to convey during your short tenure in the hot seat. It might help to think of an interview as a condensed sam-ple of your flying the line on a three-day trip at the airline, during which you encounter every kind of in-flight event known to pilots. From delays and mechanical problems to the unexpected assumption of a leadership role to a stubborn captain bent on busting min-imums to tight approaches, they want to determine how you would handle the situation when you're under pressure to perform. You have to convince a recruiter that you have the technical knowledge, leadership ability, social interaction

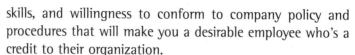

skills, and willingness to conform to company policy and procedures that will make you a desirable employee who's a credit to their organization.

Sound like a checkride? Bingo! You've just said the magic word. If you're not able to discuss your actions in an impressive manner and give examples of what you've done in the past, they'll not likely want to "fly" with you again until you've gained some additional experience.

Remember that your interview responses are actually a sales pitch for you and your abilities. If you don't give interviewers the information they need to make a decision (read: Why should we hire you?), you may find yourself interviewing over and over with nothing more than a pile of rejection letters to show for your trouble. Use your preinterview study time to prepare a unique discussion of why you want to work for that particular airline, what special qualities you possess, and how you can enhance their operation. Sell them on your skills and why, in a word, they should hire *you*.

What Interviewers Really Want

If you could read the mind of your next airline interviewer, much like Mel Gibson read the minds of women in the movie "What Women Want," you might be surprised at what reasonable and sensible thoughts keep surfacing as your interview unfolds. There would be nothing outrageous or unreasonable; just a desire to learn about who you really are and how you might act in—and react to—various events on the job.

Looking for the real you

First impressions are crucial. When you submitted your paperwork (resume, application, or both), you gave the airline a substantial self-portrait. It speaks volumes about you: your neatness, organization, attention to detail, ability to express yourself, and your interest in their company. Now you have the chance to confirm their good judgment by presenting a favorable in-the-flesh first impression. They'll be looking for good eye contact, a firm handshake, and a smile that says you're excited to be there.

Body language, an ever-present force, is a big issue during interviews. Are you growing more at ease as the interview progresses or do you remain overly nervous? Do you fidget and squirm when left unattended? Do you slouch in your chair or sit up straight, maybe even leaning forward a bit to show that you're very interested in the proceedings?

Do you have annoying personal habits that detract from an otherwise positive image?

Typical interview questions probe your background, but what the interviewer really wants to know is what you think and how you would act in various situations that inevitably arise in the cockpit.

As the interviewer looks you over, he or she might be thinking "Would I want to fly a three-day trip with this candidate?" or "Will I be able to glean enough information from this person's answers to make a relatively quick like or don't-like decision?" Typical interview questions probe your background, but what the interviewer really wants to know is what you think and how you would act in various situations that arise in the cockpit. He or she is looking for articulate, concise answers that paint a clear picture of you: the person, the pilot, the employee.

Negative characteristics

We all recall too well people we have disliked flying with. They're often poorly-dressed, lazy, complaining, unprofessional types, who aren't passonate about the job; they pay little attention to detail and tend to act disinterested, negative, defensive, and/or standoffish.

Do you have any of these characteristics? If you exhibit the slightest hint of such behavior during this showcase meeting, the interviewer can easily imagine how unpleasant it would be to fly with you: definitely not a choice for employment as a new-hire pilot.

Getting to know you better

Once you've passed the introductory/make-you-feel-at-home chitchat, the interviewer will want to discuss a subject you should know very well: yourself and your career. A typical icebreaker question might be, "How did you get started in flying?" This question can help you both get acquainted and establish some common ground.

Your job is to paint a good picture of yourself and how you came to be here today. Because employment applications tend to be rather dry documents, this is a test to see if you can make your personal history come to life in an interesting narrative. Show some sparkle and enthusiasm. Peak the interviewer's interest and make him or her want to hear more by planning your spiel to provide lively answers to many of the standard questions about education, flight training, military service (if any), and job progressions.

When you have finished your story, the interviewer will probe other areas of concern. You may be asked to recount a time when you encountered a specific set of circumstances that all pilots have experienced at some point. The focus will be on scenarios that can arise in the multipilot environment such as lack of leadership, poor decisions by captains, inability to be assertive, sexual harassment, and working together under difficult situations.

Interviewers also have areas of general interest, including technical qualifications, dedication to a pilot career, policy and procedures, leadership, and social interaction. As they listen to you, they hope not only to get to know you better but also to see you demonstrate the attributes you possess in each of these subject areas.

Expressing yourself in a succinct manner is important. Being articulate and to the point can translate into how well you would write up a mechanical problem in the airplane's logbook. Answer questions with specific examples of your past behavior, woven into a story with a beginning, middle, and an end, and then provide a summary that shows what you've learned from your experiences.

Do you measure up to your paperwork?

Let's eavesdrop on an interviewer's thoughts as you try to sell yourself during your interview. Having seen every kind of applicant imaginable, this person is hoping you'll measure up to your paperwork and be just the pilot the company is looking for.

Are you telling me what you really think or just what you think I want to hear? I know you're on your best behavior and eager not to show any flaws. How will you discuss those flaws I know you'd prefer to hide, such as bad grades, failed checkrides, firings, or violations?

I can certainly handle some bad stuff if I think you have learned something from an event and aren't trying to hide it or become defensive when I probe deeper. In the cockpit, I often have to reprimand someone, and I want to know now, before we hire you, that you can accept criticism in the constructive manner it's given.

What really turns you on? Are you faking your interest in flying? There's nothing worse than flying a month with someone who's bored with flying. Will you show me your real personality so I can judge for myself whether I think you'll fit in at our company? There has to be a bit of risk-taker in all of us, but mostly we need strong, trustworthy leaders who can make sure things are done right.

Are you hiding something from me? Have you glossed over some issues or do you have gaps in employment or education that are left unexplained? Can I believe your stories as something that really happened to you? Do I get goose bumps when I hear your scariest flying story?

How well prepared are you for my standard interview questions? Sure I'll throw you a curveball now and then, just to see if you can think on your feet (or while seated under pressure!). That's what this job is all about. We hire the extraordinary pilot, not run-of-the-mill types.

Would I put my family on an airplane flown by you? Will you be a credit to our company or does your speech or dress or do your mannerisms make me want to show you the door? Do you talk on and on, so I can't get all my questions asked in the allotted time? Or do I have to pry answers out of you word by word? Would flying with you be a pleasure or an endurance contest?

Put yourself in the interviewer's shoes. Were the tables turned, you would probably be thinking some of these same thoughts and wondering how to encourage more "truth in advertising." Trying to determine what's really inside the mind of an applicant is tough. Often interviewers have to chip way at the polite, eager façade, piece by piece. Try to help your interviewer get quickly acquainted with the real you—as if your future depended on it, as it likely does. Now, not later, is the time to show exactly who you are and how you will be an asset to the company for the rest of your flying career.

Interview Postmortem

There seems to be a special clique in aviation: a group of pilots who can't figure out why they weren't successful in passing their last major airline interview. With great flight times and hotshot answers, they figure that the interviewer must have a grudge against corporate (or regional or GA) pilots.

Needless to say, everyone who interviews can't be hired, but there are some telltale signs that become obvious when seemingly well-qualified pilots get turned down for what seems to be a trivial discrepancy or worse, for no apparent reason whatsoever. Of course, there are valid reasons, but few of them are apparent to people who have worked hard to prepare for the experience and feel that they answered every question correctly and outscored their competition by having the best of qualifications.

It's important to understand not only what is expected of you and what type of attributes you'll have to demonstrate but also why certain questions are asked and what they seek to determine. Interviewers try to cover all the problem areas that keep pilots from becoming successful, productive, company leaders.

Notice the choice of words here. The term successful presumes a high level of technical competence coupled with a positive attitude. Productive means able to deal with the environment and people to produce a top-notch product. Company refers to understanding the need for and following the specified policies and procedures of an organization as well as incorporating them into your own operating system. And finally, the emphasis on leaders is a verification that people are being hired to lead and must have the ability to do so.

What is behind certain queries?

The reason behind certain areas of inquiry—such as logbooks, applications, and college grades—is important. A company seeks not only to learn the obvious—did you fudge on your logs, are you a slob when it comes to paperwork, or does your D in math show you can't add fuel quantity gauges—but also to determine as well what kind of a person you are and how much importance you attach to these areas of great concern to an airline. Probing these subjects can also reveal your ability to deal with criticism, as well as how defensive you become when your record is scrutinized and questioned.

> A positive outlook is crucial because it helps facilitate communications both inside and outside of the cockpit and encourages productive social interaction.

Perhaps the most important trait that's closely scrutinized is general outlook on life. Is it negative or positive? Do you view an eight-ounce glass that contains four ounces of water as half full or half empty? A positive outlook is crucial because it helps facilitate communications both inside and outside of the cockpit and encourages productive social interaction.

Imagine flying a three-day trip with someone who complains constantly about everyone and everything. Nothing is ever good enough for this individual, and soon you start dreading each flight, wondering how this pilot ever got hired in the first place. Thousands of hours and numerous

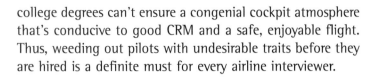

college degrees can't ensure a congenial cockpit atmosphere that's conducive to good CRM and a safe, enjoyable flight. Thus, weeding out pilots with undesirable traits before they are hired is a definite must for every airline interviewer.

How do you interact with coworkers?

With these mandates in mind, many airlines have moved their pilot-interview process from the Human Resources Department back to Flight Operations. Pilots are now hiring pilots so that those applicants who kill the joy of flying for the rest of us won't be hired just because they've filled in all the squares and seem to know all the answers.

Remember, your success as an airline pilot is deeply intertwined with how you interact with coworkers. Defensiveness is an important trait to assess during an interview because you'll be receiving lots of instruction and direction from your superiors. If you can't take advice in the spirit it's offered, recognizing we all make occasional mistakes and need to continue learning, you'll soon find yourself suffering the consequences.

A negative attitude can kill your chance for success. You may not think you sound negative, but does someone listening to your words and watching your body language feel your excitement and enthusiasm for the job? Are your descriptions so realistic that no one doubts you're honestly describing the real you? If not, why not?

If there's any doubt in your mind as to the answers to these questions, analyze carefully what message you are sending an interviewer. Airlines interview only those people they feel are qualified for employment. Your job is not only to confirm your resume or application data but also to demonstrate that you possess the many unwritten skills and abilities needed to do the job well as a new-hire pilot.

Chapter 8

INTERVIEW SECRETS

Have You Got What It Takes?

If you were trying to hire pilots, you might run the following ad: "PILOTS WANTED: Looking for good employees who lead well and get along easily with others."

Sounds like an easy order to fill, no? This advertisement is, in 15 short words, the crux of what pilot employers are looking to hire. However, finding experienced pilots who can demonstrate during an interview that they meet these requirements may be a bit more difficult than the task first appears.

What makes a good employee?

Let's start with the good employee part. It covers a lot of territory from an employer's standpoint. Do you show up for work on time, ready to do the job with a good attitude and a positive outlook? Do you follow company policies and procedures or do you try to beat the system at every opportunity?

Many questions in an interview are designed to determine your attitudes toward work in general and their company in particular. These might include, "Tell us about a time when you weren't able to live up to your own expectations at work. How did you deal with it?" (and the unspoken, "What did you learn from it?") "What do you do when you disagree with a company regulation that seems trivial and insignificant?"

You'll have to demonstrate, with examples from your working past, how you have handled these types of situations, from the ordinary to the extraordinary. Being able to

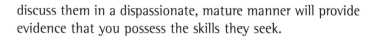

discuss them in a dispassionate, mature manner will provide evidence that you possess the skills they seek.

Are you a good leader?

The next part of our want ad, being a good leader, is the most important one for every pilot who covets the left seat. You should provide examples of what you've done in the past to demonstrate your abilities in this area, even if your PIC time is limited. What kind of leadership skills do you possess? How do you react when you're thrown into a leadership role unexpectedly? Can you learn from those around you and be selective about which qualities you adopt for your own style?

You may turn up events that demonstrate your leadership abilities by browsing through your logbook. If you're just beginning your career, keep these future needs in mind and record them as they occur. An event may be expressed as cryptically as "helped lost pilot @ CRQ" or "line of TRWs, did 180 & RON @ ICT FSS."

Don't limit yourself to flying only. Your days in scouting or volunteer work, or even a low-level managerial job you once held at a local burger joint may provide the examples you'll need to demonstrate the desired skill.

An example may not be the most momentous of events in your mind, but rather a simple one that reveals a good demonstration of your abilities. Have you ever tried to convince someone to do something they didn't particularly want to do? Lobbied to get some procedure or regulation changed? Headed a committee or group to advance a worthy cause? Or just used your head to accomplish a desired goal? All of these are bona fide illustrations of leadership skills.

Leadership can be defined in many ways. You might even think of learning to fly as a way of learning to be a leader. Think back on your own past—and keep your eyes open for future opportunities—and recall those events that show your abilities to an interviewer.

Do you get along well with others?

The last part of our calling-all-pilots announcement deals with getting along well with others—both in and outside the workplace. Because of the high-visibility nature of their jobs, pilots are expected to use myriad people skills to handle everything from a disgruntled passenger requiring special attention to a recalcitrant crew member who can't or won't do his job in an emergency situation.

Knowing how you've dealt with specific situations in the past will give interviewers a good idea of how you'll react when confronted with the inevitable conflict situation in the cockpit. By the way, saying that you've never experienced anything like this is *not* believable and will make recruiters wonder how much effort you put into your interview preparation.

Start preparing now.

Now that you know some of the areas you'll be expected to discuss in a believable manner during a pilot interview, you can start to prepare yourself for this often intimidating eventuality. You've worked hard to accumulate the required certificates, ratings, and flight time. In the same vain, you should prepare a detailed plan to demonstrate your intangible abilities.

The three basic areas of concern—being a good employee, being a good leader, and interacting well with others—are all ones you've dealt with on some level in your past. The key is to catalog in your own mind any events that clearly demonstrate your abilities in these areas. You'll want to set the scene in a few short words, describe what happened, and then say what you did about it. Tell a story, a simple three-step narrative to answer situational questions—it's exactly what an interviewer would like to hear. Relax and smile as you talk, and you'll soon find that "want ad" describing the real you.

Selling Yourself:
Sing Your Own Praises

"Tell us about yourself." It's a seemingly innocent statement but one that often strikes terror into the hearts of
pilots during an airline interview. To demystify the expectation, let's talk about how to reply and what to include in
your discussion.

First of all, consider why you're being asked this question. The most obvious reason is that the interviewer(s)
would like to get a feel for just who you are and why you're
sitting there before them today. They've read your application and/or resume and would like to have you make the
documents come alive with your own vivid rendition of your
personal life and work history.

It's also a chance for them to see how articulate you are
when discussing a subject with which you're very familiar—
yourself. Interviews, like some in-flight emergencies, can be
some of life's most stressful situations. If you can be put at
ease by discussing a familiar subject, hopefully you'll relax
and begin revealing the real person they hope to hire. I say
"hope to hire" because no one, least of all airlines, bother to
interview people they don't want to hire.

Reveal your best attributes

Everyone starts out with a positive opportunity. Your
paperwork has told them you have their stated minimums

and that you're worth interviewing. They hope you'll live up to and perhaps exceed those qualifications during your interview. Now it's your turn to show them how well you can do their job by discussing what you've done in the past and how you will fit in with their corporate culture. This is your opportunity to sell yourself by revealing who you are and what you have to offer.

Before we go any further, I'll ask you to consider one important factor. Most pilots, despite their legendary large egos, have a terrible time showing excitement and enthusiasm during an interview. You may sound blasé when you tell your fellow pilots how you dealt with three airborne emergencies in the space of a 20-minute flight from Outback to Big Town. However, an airline interview is *not* the time to be suave and cool about your background and accomplishments.

Now *is* the time to sing your own praises and get excited about the things you've achieved during your aviation career. Be proud of your achievements and describe them with the proper amount of awe, respect, and gratitude to demonstrate that you're passionate about and proud of your flying career to date.

Be proud of your achievements and describe them with the proper amount of awe, respect, and gratitude to demonstrate that you're passionate about and proud of your flying career to date.

How to tell your story

So just how do you tell your story and what should it include? One important guideline is your resume, the other, your application. If the interviewer has only one of these documents in front of him, make your summary revolve around the dates and events shown on that paperwork. Your job is to breathe life into the paper events; make them jump off the page and capture the interviewer's full attention and interest.

Fill in all the gaps and link your various life events together while simultaneously showing the blood, sweat, tears, and money you've expended in your quest for a pilot career. If, for example, you didn't do stellar college work but spent all your time at the airport washing planes in exchange for flight time, tell them about it so they understand you've made some sacrifices to get where you are today. Emphasize your positive aspects and downplay any negative ones; this is your chance to direct the focus toward your strong points and other abilities.

Before an interview, outline your sales pitch by listing 10 events in your life that were important to your development as a person and a pilot. Opposite each item, note why you've chosen to include it. If you can't show its importance in your own personal, professional, or educational advancement, you may want to delete it in favor of something that will have more impact. Your tell-us-about-yourself answer should be a thumbnail sketch of your pilot career that shows how you became interested in flying, what your education and training are, and what you've done to achieve your aviation goals.

Breathe life into your story

A brief description of your upbringing (and family, if you so choose) and personal interests can help give the interviewer a feeling for the real you. One pilot we know was concerned about stating the real reason for his career choice lest it sound too heart wrenching. His brother had been killed in an airplane crash, and he knew his mom would never forgive him if he embarked on an aviation career. The way in which he chose to start flying and how he described it to an interviewer gained him more respect and admiration than any four-year degree or type rating could have. Never underestimate the power of revealing the truth.

It's important to discuss significant accomplishments in your life with a here's-what-I'm-proud-of attitude. If you've received special recognition or performed a community service that doesn't appear in your paperwork, describe it to demonstrate what others who know you well think of you and your abilities. Working your way through college or flight school deserves special mention, as does completing a course or rating in less than the normal time.

Practice your spiel so you can comfortably deliver it in two to three minutes. Don't try to preanswer questions you think they'll ask; instead present a unique, interesting, and concise description of your strong points. Impress them with your ability to think and speak clearly, a difficult task for anyone, particularly during a high-pressure job interview. A good presentation, coupled with a pleasant, genuine smile and a relaxed attitude will go a long way toward convincing them your application deserves their special attention.

Technical Knowledge:
An Interview Must

Learning how to interview at an airline is both a skill and an art. Many pilot applicants concentrate their efforts on the more intangible areas of their careers, forgetting how important it is to review the basic technical data that lies at the very heart of their aviation knowledge.

Every professional pilot should own a good ATP manual, a current copy of the FARs applicable to their type of flying, the latest AIM, as well as books on aviation weather and CRM. Many of the areas that are covered during interview questioning come directly from the ATP written exam, including weather, charts, airport data, regs, and aircraft systems. Although you can't be expected to know everything in the manuals, you should have a good working knowledge of pertinent subjects that allows you to discuss each topic briefly. If you're uncertain about the answer to a question, at least provide a reference as to where you'd go to research the topic.

Review all your aircraft.

Pilots who fly more than one type of airplane frequently ask: "Which aircraft am I expected to know and in how much detail?" Look through your logbook and determine which twins you have flown the most and which aircraft you are currently flying. If you list several different types, then study each one in detail, with emphasis on your present equipment, so you can respond to questions normally found on an FAA oral test. These might include procedures for an in-flight engine shutdown, emergency gear extension, engine start sequence, and basic statistics on the aircraft systems. As in a checkride oral, just answer each question with a good general description. If the interviewer wants more information, he'll ask for it.

Although you can't be expected to know everything in the manuals, you should have a good working knowledge of pertinent subjects that allows you to discuss each topic briefly. If you're uncertain about the answer to a question, at least provide a reference as to where you'd go to research the topic.

Do you present the image of a knowledgeable pilot who can provide need-to-know data in a clear, concise manner? Whether your current aircraft is a C-172 or a Gulfstream IV, you should be able to give accurate systems details to convince interviewers of your professional outlook. Don't be embarrassed that you've not had an opportunity to fly faster, bigger ships—instead, dazzle them with what you do know and have learned in your quest to move up.

Terms and regulations you should be familiar with

You may encounter questions that are far above your current experience, just to see if you've taken the time to read and study subjects beyond your present certificate level. A thorough knowledge of the AIM is invaluable. Many topics for questioning will come from its various sections, and now—not when you get the interview call—is the time to reread and study everything from abbreviations (What's MAA?) to runway lights (How far apart are they?) to holding speeds and entries, wake turbulence avoidance, and lost communications procedures when IFR. When you're questioned about specific procedures, give the textbook answer, not what you would actually do in real life. Interviewers want to know that you've implanted those standards in your brain and can recite them verbatim.

As you read and study the AIM, keep a copy of the FARs nearby. You're expected to know the regs that pertain to your type of operation. If you're currently flight instructing, then be ready to discuss everything from student endorsements to license requirements and Part 135 rules for the new commercial pilot.

Regional pilots are expected to know a correspondingly larger amount of information. If your current equipment flies in the Flight Levels, then you should brush up on your high altitude systems, meteorology, and physiology. Everyone should have a good working knowledge of METARs and TAFs and be able to read and decode the basic information quickly and easily.

Can you do math problems in your head?

Your ability to do math problems in your head is another favorite testing area. If you fly 21 miles in 3 minutes, how fast are you going? If your aircraft can dump fuel at the rate of 2500 lbs/minute, how long will it take to dump 35,000 lbs. of fuel? What's reciprocal of 346 degrees? Using a 3-to-1 ratio, when should you leave FL330 to cross 30 DME from the VOR at 12,000 feet? The solutions to these questions can be tough under the best of conditions. Throw in the pressure of a job interview and many pilots find their brains turning to mush.

I have two suggestions for dealing with this type of question. First, reduce the math problem to a known quantity that can be handled easily. If the question concerns speed, remember that 6-minute units can easily be converted to hours by adding a zero. Or 1- and 10-minute units convert to hours by multiplying the quantity by 60 or 6, respectively. Second, verbalize the problem out loud to show your thought process. You may well get points for using the right method, even if you come up with the wrong answer.

How are you with instrument charts?

Your knowledge of instrument chart details may also be tested. The Jeppesen Airway Manual has an excellent introduction describing all of their charts, including departure, approach, and en route. If you've not looked at a government-issued chart since you took your Instrument Written Exam, now's the time to review their procedures and refresh your memory on how their charts differ and where to find specific data such as nonstandard alternate minimums and VOT frequencies.

You should be able to thoroughly brief an instrument approach procedure—any approach they select—and don't forget to turn the Jeppesen chart over (or ask to see the runway diagram if it's not presented to you), in order to discuss the runway environment and your taxi route to the terminal if you normally park there. Again, your knowledge should be commensurate with your experience and present operating environment and leave no question as to your technical competence.

Meteorology and safety

Meteorology, the universal pilot's nemesis, is another weak spot often chosen for testing. Describe the stages of a thunderstorm. What's the standard lapse rate? How does clear ice differ from rime ice? Discuss the formation of radiation versus advection fog. What altitude does the 500 MB chart represent? What's an occluded front? Define isobars, isotachs, and isotherms. OK, you get the idea. A thorough review of *Aviation Weather* or a similar publication will be very helpful in preparing for this line of questioning.

Safety concerns are also likely targets for interviewers. You may encounter questions on types of hydroplaning, deicing fluids and procedures, avoidance of wake turbulence, determination of density altitude, runway markings, and aircraft approach categories. Of particular interest are the V-speed definitions (V1, VR, V2) and how they relate to the balanced field concept. Another favorite is how to determine a Visual Descent Point (VDP) on a straight-in non-precision instrument approach, both with and without DME.

By now your head must be reeling from information overload. Perhaps the suggestion to start your studying early has finally begun to take hold. Knowing what you could face during your upcoming interview is much better than finding out too late to prepare, or worse, during the interview itself. Begin your preparation now or intensify your normal ongoing refresher training, to lower your blood pressure and increase your knowledge and confidence level for your upcoming interview.

Career Commitment: Does Yours Measure Up?

When queried about their commitment, most pilots will tell you "Of course I'm committed to this career! Why else would I be working at this (fill-in-the-blank) flying job?" But are they really? Do you know what commitment means, particularly as used by an airline interviewer grilling you on just about everything you've done during your flying career?

Start back at the beginning and recall your motivations as you took your first flying lessons. Fun, excitement, a challenge, a sense of fulfillment—just what was it that got you started? Then, did you progress at your own direction or was someone else pushing you along?

Is there enough passion in your quest?

Airlines want to know what's behind the proper navy blue suit, shined shoes, and glad-handing smile. Do you have the passion to succeed when the going gets tough? One pilot we know was hired many years ago when investigative interview techniques weren't so highly developed. After an unsuccessful checkout as a first officer on the Boeing 727, he returned to the line as a second officer or flight engineer, and, after a second failed training cycle in the right seat, eventually left the company. Later, after in-depth questioning, the pilot admitted that flying had never

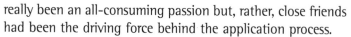

really been an all-consuming passion but, rather, close friends had been the driving force behind the application process.

Money is another factor that can make or break seeming dedication to a pilot career. Is your passion fueled by the dollars you perceive to be waiting for you along the yellow-brick road to airborne stardom? If your application shows continual movement from one job to another primarily for monetary reasons, you'll not likely find happiness as an airline pilot. You need an intrinsic satisfaction with flying that overshadows financial remuneration—whatever your pay is.

And what about the personal sacrifices? How do you feel about years of hard work, poor pay, long hours, and maybe continual rejection for jobs that seem to fall right into your best buddy's lap? Are you tired of the lack of progress and figure someone owes you a big reward after all you've given up to bask in this questionable aviation limelight? How you view and describe your past, career planning, and development will alert a sharp interviewer to whether you'll handle their pilot position with eager enthusiasm or blasé boredom, even if it's masked initially by a cheery smile and "Yes, sir!" attitude.

Use examples from your own past rather than a hypothetical "Here's what I would do" to demonstrate that you possess the "right stuff" an airline seeks. Remember that telling someone what you have done in a particular situation is infinitely more credible to a trained ear. Any interviewer will be wary of someone who demonstrates little passion or personal sacrifice in their past history.

Questions like, "Why do you want to work for our airline?" and "Why should we hire you (when we have so many better qualified applicants)?" are tests not only of your knowledge and insight but also of your passion and performance. Make sure your answers clearly demonstrate your above average skill, strong commitment to aviation, long-term career planning, keen interest in the pilot profession, and continuing efforts to stay current and up-to-date on aviation developments.

Think carefully about your motivations.

Such questions as "Would you commute?" or "How do you feel about a second-officer or flight-engineer position?" can easily pierce your interview armor and reveal disturbing trends and potential problems, particularly if you have a significant history as a PIC or management pilot. The interviewer naturally wonders how you'll fare as a small fish in a big pond when your history shows your preference for the reverse.

Anticipate these queries and think carefully about your real motivations for accepting your previous flying positions. Answer questions with not only what you would do but also the reasoning behind your decision, revealing your planning, insight, and careful analysis of your specific situation. Let them know that you'll bring to their organization a variety of talents in addition to your piloting skills, and that these assets would make you a much-desired addition to their pilot seniority list.

Your commitment to a flying career is probably the most closely scrutinized attribute of all those areas probed at an interview. Wrongly phrasing an answer or too quickly replying to a question can damage your credibility as your comments are reviewed during the post-interview evaluation phase.

Describing your passion for flying should evoke emotions of understanding in an interviewer's heart (yes, they do have them!). Make sure that your speech is animated and your eyes light up when you talk about your past. Relive for them the fun, excitement, challenge, and dedication that distinguish you from other applicants who may have similar credentials but lack the spirit and soul that you possess. Convince them that you will contribute your assets to their airline, both in and out of the cockpit.

Playing by the Rules

It's how you play the game, not whether you win or lose. No doubt you've heard this adage many times before, but it's particularly true in aviation, given all its rules and regulations, written and unwritten. Learning to play by the rules will be one of the most important aspects of your career, regardless of where or how you live out your flying aspirations.

As you venture into the formal world of flying, you're going to encounter a lot of scrutiny of your ability to deal with the structure and protocol of commercial flying. You'll find prospective employers probing your tolerance for and adherence to rules, whether they are the commonplace written variety or the less obvious unspoken ones.

Do you conform to policy and procedures?

Policy and procedures (P & Ps) are the general terms that interviewers use. These include not only your willingness to relate to routine operations in a manner that's consistent with existing regulations but also your ability to conform to established P & Ps. They're going to be delving deeply as well into how well you work within the very structured environment of an airline or corporate job.

Are you the "end-run" type who reacts negatively to directives from higher management? Do you become resentful when you don't agree with a corporate policy or procedure, figuring management is really the problem? Maybe you're a hot-shot pilot who spends most of your time try-ing to beat the system. If any of these examples sound familiar, remember that this area of scrutiny is of special interest to pilot employers because of the by-the-book nature of our profession, particularly since the events of September 11, 2001.

What are they probing for?

Remember those questions on the application about sick days you've taken during the past year? This could also read, "Are you a conscientious employee who has a good atten-dance record?" How about moving violations on your DMV record? The more tickets you have, the less likely a company will be interested in your qualifications. They assume that what you do when confronted with one set of rules reflects how you will regard other sets, namely, their own company regulations as well as the FARs.

General questions can range from "Tell us about a time you didn't comply with company policy and procedures" to "When did you follow the rules even though you thought they were wrong or unfair?" Their goal is to see if you have a well-developed sense of compliance, laced with a good dose of common sense. You should choose examples from your background that show you understand why the rules exist and that you can conform to them even if you disagree. You might include some that demonstrate you're sufficient-ly proactive to suggest changes that make rules more effec-tive. In a word, when you see a wrong, you try to right it.

Good answers to a noncompliance question might indi-cate the occasional bending of rules for passenger safety or operational necessity. Perhaps your present employer does not adhere to a safety procedure you think is important—such as tying down training aircraft after every flight or per-sonally escorting passengers through a ramp area that is under construction. Describing an instance in which you took the initiative to go the extra mile will likely impress

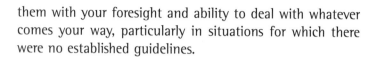

them with your foresight and ability to deal with whatever comes your way, particularly in situations for which there were no established guidelines.

Do you ever break the rules?

Beware of tricky questions that seemingly ask you to swear undying allegiance to the almighty rulebook. "Have you ever broken an FAR?" is a typical example. You figure you are opening a can of worms if you say yes and are not credible if you say no. So what's the correct answer? It's one that is believable and realistic at the same time. Everyone has broken an FAR at one time or another, so the real question is, did you do it deliberately? Are you such a goody-goody that no one will want to fly with you lest they find you constantly correcting and scolding them? Or, can you discuss your thoughts on the subject openly and honestly and admit you've probably broken a number of regulations unintentionally during your career, but you value your licenses and wouldn't jeopardize them with any intentional violations.

All pilot interviewers wish they could fly with each applicant to see just how that person reacts in a variety of situations. Because they can't, you have to provide them with some real insight into how you deal with both the ordinary and extraordinary events that make commercial flying the desirable profession it is today.

Be sure your answers reveal the real you and your honest desire to do the job to the best of your ability, according to established rules and regulations. You'll find that, ultimately, your attitude toward policy and procedure has much more to do with your chances of getting hired than does your ability to answer every question with what you think they want to hear. Being able to play the game well IS important, and that's what determines whether you'll get the chance to make the team.

Leadership Skills:
Are Yours up to Par?

When was the last time you assumed a leadership role? What are the qualities of a good leader? Tell us about a time when your leadership skills failed. Describe your leadership style and give examples to illustrate your techniques. You probably know that leadership is one of the seven important areas that airline interviewers scrutinize. (The other six are technical ability; dedication to a pilot career; adherence to policy and procedures; decision making and problem solving; relationships and social interaction; and appearance.) You should have a good idea of your leadership strengths and weaknesses and be able provide examples that show you have those "captain qualities" they're seeking.

Just what is a leader?

Many pilots scratch their heads when asked to discuss their leadership abilities, not knowing exactly what the interviewer wants to hear. Well, let's back up a bit and talk about just what leadership entails and how to find some examples in your own background. If you are a leader, you are self-confident and inspire self-confidence in others; you project personal dynamism and know how to speak in a way that moves others to action; you're good at nurturing and coaching others, helping them to be more effective and creative.

Probably the most important quality of a leader is the ability to build teamwork. Many interviewers see this as a sign of a sure winner, someone who is definite captain material. After all, isn't the seamless operation of a complex aircraft an example of true teamwork? If they hire you to fly their aircraft, they want to know you'll be able to success-fully lead your whole crew, making each flight a smooth-running successful operation.

Are you a potential captain?

Airlines hire captains—not first or second officers—pilots who are capable of doing that job from day one. Your job dur-ing the interview is to show them you possess the potential to perform a captain's tasks. Tell them about the teams you've led in the past, whether playing sports or slinging hash. Speak confidently about how you influenced others to follow your recommendations, perhaps for a charitable cause, in a class-room, at a conference table, or in the cockpit. Think about a time when you undertook a project to improve or enhance something in your workplace. Note what steps you followed, how you convinced others to help you in your endeavor, and what the results were once the job was complete.

You can follow this simple three-step procedure: set the scene, describe what happened, and then tell what you did about the situation and/or learned from it. If you're having trouble finding examples, review your job history with each of your previous employers and ask yourself what things you accomplished during your tenure. Don't overlook the little things. Maybe your influence and hard work resulted in a simple solution for a complex office procedure, or perhaps you saved the company money by instituting a new way of handling a situation. Organizing local pilots to donate their time in classrooms or leading a crusade for better airport safety conditions also demonstrates leadership. Think of times when you've made suggestions that inspired some group, somewhere, to work effectively together.

Another place to look for leadership examples is in your logbook. The notes section for each flight should contain some good reminders about times you have flown with someone who has been influenced by your coaching. CFIs are particularly fortunate in that they've probably nurtured and influenced numerous pilots and can expand on several incidents to demonstrate their leadership abilities.

Describe what you have done.

Interviewers want to see concrete examples of what you have done, not just hypothetical descriptions of how you would lead if asked to do so. Many of their questions will probe your leadership ability in the policy and procedures areas as well as decision making and problem solving. Your leadership abilities will be tested during your very first days with an airline and they'll want to know that you can fit right in by inspiring and motivating others to fulfill their goals. Project an I-care-more-about-us-than-about-me attitude to demonstrate that you can move others to action.

To describe your leadership style, use examples that show how you lead, whether by example, pitching in and working right along with the group, taking the first step, or shouldering the biggest burden to get people started. Relate how you establish trust and build teamwork by fostering creativity and providing verbal as well as nonverbal motivation. If you'd like to read a good book on the subject, I recommend Andrew J. Dubrin's *10 Minute Guide to Leadership* (Macmillan Spectrum/Alpha Books).

In a nutshell, you must convince your interviewer(s), in a rather short period of time, that you are a creative problem solver who uses your imagination, enthusiasm, and positive energy to motivate and inspire others to do their very best. Give them concise examples, however basic or simple, that will sell them on your leadership abilities and make them eager to have you join their airline's pilot team.

Plays Well with Others

"Plays well with others," sounds like something your kindergarten teacher might have noted on your first report card after seeing how you interacted socially with other children. Now, twenty or thirty years later, you're still being graded on how you get along with others. Some things never change.

Getting along is, in a nutshell, what airline flying is all about. I can't think of any other endeavor that requires such a monumental amount of teamwork. Let's start inside the cockpit, where you'll work with other pilots, mechanics, and controllers. Move on to the passenger cabin, where you'll interface with flight attendants, passengers, and gate agents, as well as law enforcement and medical personnel. Finally, step outside the airplane, where you'll be coordinating with everyone from rampers (the insider's term for baggage handlers and airplane service personnel) to airport authorities to postal workers and funeral directors. Think about trying to do just your own flying chores—and see how far an airliner will move without the army of workers who attend to every imaginable detail and some you haven't even thought of!

The importance of interpersonal skills

CRM, or lack thereof, has become a keystone to accident prevention. Take, for example, the crash of a DC-10 in

Mexico City during the late 1970s. Accident reports showed that the first officer was extremely annoyed with the other pilot and he failed to speak up when he saw a potential safety hazard. His lack of input, when the captain lined up for landing on a runway that was closed for construction, was certainly one contributing cause of this tragic accident.

Because interpersonal skills can be crucial to your success as an airline pilot, they'll be probed during an interview. An interviewer has to gain some in-depth knowledge of how you react to others and what you've done to solve situations that involve personality conflicts—especially inside the cockpit.

> An interviewer has to gain some in-depth knowledge of how you react to others and what you've done to solve situations that involve personality conflicts—especially inside the cockpit.

An interviewer may ask you to describe how you handled a personality conflict in the cockpit. Too often, we see pilots trying to answer this question in a generic, nonspecific manner that tells the listener nothing about the prospective pilot's ability to resolve quickly what could become a life-threatening event. Telling them you flew with a grouchy captain who later softened up over dinner does nothing to demonstrate your skills at actively solving the problem. Describe, instead, how you initiated reconciliation on the second leg of your four-day trip by asking the other pilot what you could do to make the cockpit a better workplace. Demonstrate that your strong desire to get along with others and communicate openly, regardless of who's at fault, has existed in the past and will continue to play an important part in your personal cockpit repertoire in the future.

Communicating effectively with a style that builds credibility and respect is going to be an important key to your flight-deck success. Can you relate to others in an honest, straightforward, mature manner? Your stories should demonstrate specific instances in which you interacted with your coworkers in a friendly, courteous manner and treated them with respect.

Interviewers are on the lookout for these warning signs: interrupting others, evading responses to questions, acting in an arrogant or know-it-all manner, and, probably the number one red flag, being defensive in any way. As you might have guessed, a defensive pilot is in constant denial and represents a real threat to aviation safety. No airline wants to hire this type of person and will go to great lengths to uncover this quality during the screening process.

Typical questions will range from how you would deal with a captain who appears to have been drinking to handling one who appears to be busting DH on a tight approach. Listening effectively and communicating clearly, as well as having a "thick skin" when a situation requires it, can be keys to a successful airline pilot career. You must demonstrate that you possess this skill by giving a concise description of how you overcame communication obstacles to quickly establish a comfortable rapport with coworkers.

Handling errors

"Hey, Captain, I can't believe I missed that hydraulic leak—I did a thorough walk-around inspection. I'm sure glad those rampers said something to us. In the future, I'll have to double check these hydraulic thing-a-ma-jigs before—and after—my preflight." This is the proper way to handle those inevitable errors we all make. You are acknowledging your mistake and indicating you're concern about a situation that is supposed to be in your area of expertise. You are taking responsibility for your actions and working to identify and correct any problems before they grow into large ones. Someone listening to this rehash of the problem will realize that you're serious about your responsibilities and not trying to duck a problem or brush it off with a don't-blame-me attitude.

Keeping a high score

An airline pilot's working life could easily be described as nothing more than one big group effort. It's a game whose successful outcome is entirely dependent on the contributions of all the players. I like to compare each of my trips to a pinball game in which I start with a score of 1,000 points. For each error, omission, or screw-up, I lose 10 points. I try to help my coworkers minimize their points lost as well. The object, of course, is to complete the flight with the highest possible score.

Everyone's performance in life is scored in some way or other. As an airline pilot, you'll find that your actions are watched much more closely than those of other employees. Because your ability to get along with others can be a matter of life and death, rest assured it's going to be of great interest to anyone who's scrutinizing your pilot credentials during the hiring process.

CHAPTER 9

AIRLINE FLYING

Flying the Simulator: It's Not an Airplane!

Many simulators don't even come close to replicating the airplane they're supposed to simulate. But as we talk with interviewing pilots, it's clear that many of them aren't aware of just how important simulator evaluation is during the hiring process.

Let's start back at the point when you were working on your instrument rating. You probably realized that it was to be the most important rating of your career and that you shouldn't skimp on the basics. Developing a good instrument panel scan is a must for the professional pilot and that's only the beginning. Keeping that scan in good repair is a constant battle for everyone, from the newly-minted IFR pilot to the seasoned airline captain. Like it or not, your scan will depart the area with surprising rapidity, once you let up on the continuous practice that's required to keep it sharp.

If you're just getting into aviation, you should pay close attention during your instrument training and plan carefully for the ongoing maintenance of your skills. As you progress into bigger airplanes, the use of simulators will become increasingly important. You'll be expected to demonstrate your IFR skills on every type of simulator, from a basic tabletop model to a full-motion machine that may have been built before you were born.

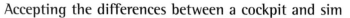

Accepting the differences between a cockpit and sim

Dealing with the simulator phenomena is very much a mindset. Complaining that the sim you've been given to fly doesn't replicate the airplane is a waste of time. Your job is to know how to fly a simulator. In the process, you'll have to disregard the make and model hype that can lead you into thinking you're flying an airplane—you're not! Think of the experience as an exercise designed to test your instant accommodation skills.

Most airline simulators do a good job of replicating a cockpit, but often their flying characteristics leave a lot to be desired. You may think they're a duplicate at first, but after you've flown the real McCoy for a while and return to the sim, you'll curse its insensitivity—or over sensitivity—noting that the airplane flies much better than this beast.

Passing a sim test is a prerequisite to being hired.

Your job as a pilot applicant is to pass a sim ride, and doing so can take as much practice as, if not more than, what you've expended in studying for the written tests or interviews. Even if you're now employed as a pilot, don't expect to pass a sim ride without any preparation. Spend some time refreshing your sim skills. We've seen too many pilots work hard on their interview techniques and brush off the sim check with a "No problem, I'm current." Later, we learn that they passed the interview portion and then lost it when the "box" ate their lunch, so to speak.

Flying regularly is good practice for flying airplanes, not simulators. Flying a sim well and passing your new-hire checkride requires focused training with a good instructor. It's fine to amuse yourself by dabbling with a PC-based desktop sim or jumping into a transport-type simulator, but beware of thinking that because you flew it around the patch a few times, you'll ace the checkride.

Spend the time—usually a minimum of two to three hours—and money to get some real training that includes basic IFR maneuvers, approaches, emergencies, and unusual attitudes. Although many of these events may not occur during your checkride, your thorough preparation will give you the confidence necessary to handle any unfamiliar scenarios your evaluator may give you.

Become thoroughly acquainted with your sim and its instruments. One pilot we know was unfamiliar with the sky pointer type of attitude indicator and became disoriented during his pre-hire check, ruining an otherwise well-flown ride. Instead of receiving thumbs up, he was told he could reapply six months later. Had he spent some time in a structured practice environment, his results might have been an offer of a class date.

Keep your simulator skills sharp.

Even if you fly often, practice in a sim is worth the investment. For example, if you're giving scenic tours and find most of your flights are VFR or if you're giving lots of instruction, even though it may be IFR dual, you'll definitely want to become sim current before any pre-hire checkride.

You don't have to rent a DC10 simulator just because the airline uses one for testing their applicants. Save your money and use a PC-type sim to keep up your scan. Then, when you're comfortable and current, buy a few hours of time from an instructor who's proficient at training in a stand-alone sim prior to your testing situation.

Simulators aren't airplanes but they do provide many opportunities that airplanes can't. Flying in any kind of weather, any time, any place, to any destination can be of great benefit to pilots who may not have the opportunities to experience a wide range of flight conditions. Ultimately, we all need to keep our simulator skills sharp. If you've never flown a sim, now is the time to begin preparing for that coveted phone call or letter inviting you to demonstrate those skills you've so wisely practiced.

You're Hired! Now What?

"Help!" read the e-mail from a Canadian female pilot, "I've been hired at an airline and don't have any idea what to expect or how to prepare for training. Can you help me?" Well, yes and no. There's a wealth of information she'll have to learn as well as a huge amount she already knows, and there are numerous resources she can turn to for assistance.

Let's start by talking about what is expected of any new airline pilot. Unlike a type-rating course or recurrent training session for which you (or your employer) are paying, you're now being paid to learn and expected to produce results. Some of your best advance work will be clearing your emotional decks so you can concentrate on the tasks at hand.

Take care of household chores, clean up any details that lurk among your I'll-do-it-later paperwork, and get ready to be really busy, with no time to do anything but study, sleep, study, grab a quick bite, study, and then study some more. There will not be enough hours in the day, and the ongoing pressure will be enormous. Surviving training will be nothing like you ever imagined.

How will you handle it all?

The barrage of information is unbelievable. Where are you expected to find all those numbers and details? Why do you have to know the power source for every item on the panel? You're expected to study abnormal procedures, memorize limitations and checklists, and review flows and sequences. How will you handle it all? The answer is systematically and methodically, dividing up your available time to give some coverage to all subjects so you have a working knowledge of each topic and can fill in the gaps later.

Think back on each of your ratings and the preparation it took to successfully complete those checkrides. Your current job will be much the same, except the learning is going to be highly compressed into very full days and too short nights.

To accelerate your learning, begin by reviewing a good ATP manual, giving special attention to the FARs (or regs for your individual country, as the case may be) and your particular type of operation. Look carefully at oxygen regulations and how they differ from not-for-hire flying. What about the requirements for continuing an instrument approach once inside the marker? Alternate airport regs, take off limitations, and holding procedures are also good areas to study.

If you're not sharp at reading METARs and TAFs, review them until you're comfortable picking out standard data, such as visibility for takeoff planning and forecast ceilings for alternate airport requirements. Much of this data will be your responsibility, even though little or no mention may be made of it in class, so now is the time to review it.

Sharpen rusty skills.

If you're feeling rusty in your study skills, pick up a good how-to text and relearn those techniques you used to take for granted. If you can get a copy of the airplane training manual before class begins, read ahead to preview your upcoming workload. Do keep in mind that if you're learning a new-generation aircraft, some of the old study techniques may not be applicable to computer-based training. You may have no ground school to attend, no instructor to query. Be sure you know what's expected of you and ask plenty of questions—up front when you're just beginning your training session.

If your instrument skills are rusty, get current in whatever is available to you, be it a PC sim or your friend's C172. You're starting your new job as a flying pilot, and it's important to have a good IFR scan when you begin the simulator or airplane training. If necessary, read up on any special equipment you may encounter (such as HSIs and RMIs) in case you haven't used them before. Wasting valuable study time on should-have-known items can put you way behind your classmates and seriously endanger your timely completion.

Get help from another pilot.

Probably your best preparation will come from networking. Find another pilot who has recently completed the course you're taking and talk with him or her regarding the training experience at your new airline. Don't be shy about admitting what you don't know and asking questions—lots of them! Remember that everyone was in your place when they started as a new-hire pilot. Your arrival signals that they are moving up the seniority ladder and they'll be glad to help if you make your request with an I'm-eager-to-learn attitude.

> Don't be shy about admitting what you don't know and asking questions—lots of them! Remember that everyone was in your place when they started as a new-hire pilot.

Accept the fact that there's never going to be enough time to learn it all. Some information you'll just have to memorize and leave the understanding until later. Do your best, maintain a positive mental attitude, and ask for help as soon as you think you need it, rather than waiting until the day before your checkride. You've been hired because they know you can do the job; now show them you're willing, able, and ready to do whatever it takes to ensure the successful completion of your training.

Ground School Starts Monday: Are You Ready?

Ground School—it's got to be one of the most exciting events in your pilot career! Instead of the haphazard, do-it-yourself style of some GA training situations, you're now going to encounter a real, formal training session that will prepare you to deal with the rigors of scheduled airline flying.

If you have previously attended a systems-oriented ground school or type-rating training at a professional learning center, you've got a pretty good idea of what lies in store for you. If not, hold on to your hat—you're in for a wild and often bumpy ride! But remember that now you're being paid to learn the material and it's not a case of your paying them to get you through the course. You have to demonstrate that you've got what it takes and can keep up with the pace and the volume of data that will be thrust upon you—in a manner that's often described as fire-hose style.

Surviving the rigors of training

Getting through ground school and the requisite tests—sometimes they're given daily—is certainly stressful. However, once you pass that milestone, you'll be faced with the ultimate high-pressure challenge: the simulator. By comparison, sim sessions make ground school look like child's play. Soon, you'll be wishing you were back in the comfort of the classroom, where the daily menu was at least cut and dried and, although hydraulics may have been an eyelid drooper, you knew the basics of what was on the agenda.

But let's back up a moment and discuss some prerequisites for surviving the ordeal the airlines call training. Depending on your background, the experience can range from routine ("Ho hum, here we go again.") to roller-coaster-like in its ability to unhinge even the best of pilots. Pilots whose backgrounds include a lot of hands-on flying in high-performance aircraft will do well in this training environment. An example would be the night-freight pilot who hand flies hard IFR approaches regularly, makes frequent weather decisions, and is used to the pressure of keeping a schedule. This person is accustomed to the juggling act and is now delighted to have a job that allows him to work some daylight hours and boasts real employee perks such as pass travel, health insurance, and perhaps retirement benefits.

Ground school in particular—and training in general—will be tougher for general-aviation pilots with low multiengine time. CFIs, for example, can find themselves fighting to keep up with the training if they've spent most of their time instructing without much hands-on flying. A crucial factor, their instrument scan, is likely based on the age-old instructor's "scan and peek" system, in which case they'll find themselves very rusty when it comes to a minimums approach or an ADF holding pattern.

IFR currency can, of course, be easily remedied by some concentrated hood sessions combined with using a PC sim or other training device. What is very difficult to overcome, however, can be a lack of basic knowledge that's unfortunately all too common among GA pilots with little or no systems background. Not knowing what a pack is, what a heat exchanger does, or how an accumulator works can severely hamper your progress in absorbing some very technical classroom material. Electrical-systems knowledge (or lack thereof) can be the most crippling for anyone trying to understand schematic diagrams that bear little resemblance to what they've seen in GA owner's manuals.

The importance of advance preparation

Advance preparation is the key to a successful transit through your company's new-hire training. Begin by recognizing that this milestone in your aviation career requires a concentrated amount of time and effort. Prepare your family and friends for the six-to-eight-week absence it will require and clean up any loose ends on the home front. Pay bills, complete medical chores (be sure your FAA physical does not come due during your training), and deal with any business that might distract you from concentrating on your primary target. You will have to focus completely on training.

> Advance preparation is the key to a successful transit through your company's new-hire training.

Preparation falls into two categories: systems knowledge and instrument proficiency. Your systems knowledge can be further subdivided into all the material you're expected to know prior to starting ground school and your personal familiarity with aircraft systems, from basic to advanced. Think of your training as a transition to another airplane—because that's the way it will be taught—rather than moving up to a bigger airplane.

You're expected to be thoroughly familiar with all the ATP knowledge from FARs to IFR procedures, from understanding weather to approach/en route chart interpretation. A good ATP text is certainly a good place to start your review, along with copies of the regs, AIM, and the introduction to the Jeppesen Airway Manual.

If you suspect that your systems knowledge is on the skimpy side (Do you think transformer rectifiers sound like something out of Star Trek?), spend some time studying video, audio, or written texts that cover the basics of big airplane systems. Nothing you hear in ground school should come as a shock. You should have at least some familiarity with all the pieces—pneumatic, electric, hydraulic, and engine-driven—before you take the plunge.

Good instrument proficiency goes without saying. You can't survive sim training without a good IFR scan, a helpful sim partner, and an open mind. You'll make lots of mistakes, so the best plan is to learn from them and move on.

Just as you found extensive ground-school preparation to be invaluable, so will you have to adopt a keep-on-studying attitude about the sim and the flight-training events that follow it. Keep your eyes and ears open, ask for help when you need it, and don't be afraid to speak up about any concerns you have regarding your progress. Your future success as an airline pilot depends on successfully completing the rigors of this grueling ritual known as new-hire training.

Surviving New-Hire Training

It's been your dream of a lifetime—flying for an airline—and now it's finally within your grasp. You've passed the interview, the sim ride, and the physical exam, and you've finally received the call or the letter inviting you to join the next new-hire pilot class at your favorite airline.

With a new life ahead of you, you're eager to get started. You've got a whole new set of hurdles to clear, however, before you can relax and turn on the autopilot, so speak. This is no time to let your guard down; your work has just begun. But I should let you in on a little secret—there's no real end in sight. There's always one more simulator ride, one more line check, another physical exam—right up until the very end of the line at age 60. So, get used to it. Like death and taxes, you've got lots of "you-bet-your-job" events to look forward to during your airline career. Consider each one a challenge to be reckoned with, prepared for, properly executed, learned from, and, finally, put behind you until it's time to start the whole process over again for your next inevitable training session.

Preparation for the challenge ahead

Preparation entails a lot of work on your part, both mental and physical. Study and headwork are required, but your physical well-being is also an important part of succeeding at your new profession.

On previous pages I've discussed the importance of cleaning up any personal loose ends so you can devote yourself to what has been likened to "drinking from a fire hose," that is, successfully completing new-hire ground school. From mortgage payments to medical exams, be sure you've completed all those time-consuming tasks that can rob you of precious study time. Believe me, you'll need every minute you've got (and be looking for more) before you can breathe the sigh of relief that comes after you've been signed off for line flying.

Ground school, with its volumes of material to be learned, is usually preceded by several days of company indoctrination, which covers the inevitable paperwork (a never-ending chore); company policies, procedures, and benefits; FAA regulations; and safety and security data. Finally, when you think the stack of manuals can grow no higher, you'll be given the one you've been waiting for—the Airplane Flight Manual (AFM) and its associated limitations; normal, abnormal, and emergency procedures; systems descriptions; and those all-important checklists.

Some tips for surviving ground school

One difficulty in surviving training is that you often won't know what to study or in what order. Because the information will come with machine-gun rapidity, your job is to preview the material so you have some inkling of what's about to be discussed.

All airline flight manuals are set up in basically the same order, but you can get an overview by starting with the Limitations. You'll probably be required to memorize these numbers, but for now, get an idea of what the "limits" are so your reading of the data will make some sense. Next, read the descriptive chapter that explains the system in detail. Then, read through Normal Procedures and learn how this system is used in everyday operations. Follow up with a look at Abnormal Procedures and then check out the Emergency

Procedures. Once you have a good foundation in how the system is used, review any handouts or study guides and finish up with the MEL (Minimum Equipment List) to determine what's required if a component is inoperative.

The above sounds like a lot of preview work—and it is—but it's well worth the effort. You'll find the class presentation and discussion much more meaningful and easy to digest. When you know what's important to line flying (from your review the night before), you can concentrate on crucial information and ask questions in class based on your preparatory reading. You'll also find an amazing amount of important material hidden in places you never suspected. Many limitations aren't found in the Limitations section but rather in the Normal Procedures or the MEL. Knowing where to look for information you need is half the battle won and will greatly ease your anxiety as you wade through the mountain of ground-school study material.

Knowing where to look for information you need is half the battle won and will greatly ease your anxiety as you wade through the mountain of ground-school study material.

Successful completion of ground school is crucial to your advancement through the training mill. Many airlines require a minimum passing grade of 80% or better. Pilots scoring 79 or less are quietly shown the door, leaving their empty chairs as a grim reminder of what making the grade is all about. Although ground school may resemble a pressure cooker, it's nothing compared to what will follow with the CPT (cockpit procedures trainer) and simulator. Now, you not only have to draw quickly on the material you learned in ground school, but also apply it.

Becoming familiar with the cockpit

Your first exposure to the "cockpit" can range from a simulator that's not turned on, to a non-motion simulator, to a mock-up of the cockpit, to colored photos of the real thing hung on the wall to resemble your future office. Here, you'll practice "flows," or the sequence in which you'll operate various switches for each phase of flight. Learning these flow patterns in advance is extremely important. You have to quickly and accurately find the correct switch or gauge, analyze its position or reading, perform any necessary manipulation, and move on to the next item in the sequence.

When you first enter a cockpit to perform a preflight check, you'll use a specific flow pattern, just as you will before every checklist or normal procedure. Everything from checking the battery status—an all-important item for large airplanes—to providing heating or cooling has a very specific step-by-step process whose flow pattern you must learn. When you study these flows, recite each action as you physically move your hand to the specific switch and move it to the required position. The process must become second nature and something you can accomplish quickly and accurately while watching for any abnormalities.

During my new-hire training to be a Boeing 727 flight engineer or second officer, we were required to obtain 25 hours of observation time in the cockpit prior to beginning our simulator sessions. The instructors admitted that they had no time to teach normal operating procedures and that we were expected to learn them during these ACM (additional crew member) rides. So, I did lots of observing, asked questions, and became comfortable with my new environment before I had to do battle with it in the simulator.

The simulator and checkride hurdles

As you move on to simulator training, the same rules that helped you through ground school and CPT will apply to your new virtual airplane. You'll be faced with huge volumes of material to study and review before each session and will be required to know the flows associated with each procedure. As pressure mounts, keep in mind the most important rule of all: don't dwell on your mistakes! Learn from each of your errors and move on—quickly absorbing what you've done wrong and clearing your mental slate for what's to come.

Take notes during each debriefing, so you can refer to the information during your post-sim study session. Everyone makes mistakes; use them like mental locks or rights of passage that can move you on to the next level of learning. Don't let them become roadblocks that detour your concentration and plunge your performance into a downward spiral. Two pilots in my new-hire pilot class were shown the door when they failed to successfully complete their sim training. I suspect that they helped do each other in by feeding off of one another's failures.

Just when you're sure you can absorb no more, your checkride or proficiency check will loom as that last apparent hurdle. Remember, throughout your training you've been demonstrating that the company did, indeed, make a good choice when it hired you. You told them during your interview that you could successfully deal with the challenges of airline training—and now you get to prove it.

This whole procedure is quite different from the buy-a-type rating programs in which the school's job is to get you through the course. You must show you can do the job you've been hired to do. And so you will, by maintaining a positive attitude and using the knowledge you've gained through concentrated, systematic study, training, and practice.

Adapting to Life at an Airline

Occasionally we encounter pilots who have recently entered the world of commercial flying and realize that they were totally unprepared for the regimentation and control imposed by the company. In such cases, their expectations seem to diverge 180 degrees from reality, and when asked what they *did* expect, the answer is usually, "Gee, a little freedom and control over my life."

Keep in mind, as you move into any commercial operation, the key words will be *safety* and *scheduling*. Your vision of each one can vary markedly from that of your superiors. Your job is to learn their interpretations and blend them into your work.

Some of the expectations

Let's start with training. Remember that you're now being paid to learn and are expected to produce results by scheduling yourself to cram the maximum amount of technical information into your head in the minimum amount of time. You will have to review material before it's presented in class, take good notes, and absorb voluminous amounts of data.

Ground school will seem like a huge overload until you proceed to the cockpit procedures trainer (CPT) and the simulator (sim). Then, you'll wish you were back in ground school, where the expectations were simply to study material, take a test on it, and move on.

Once your systems knowledge is theoretically complete, you're off to the cockpit—a paper mock-up, a nonmoving simulator, or maybe even the real airplane—for a chance to apply your newly-acquired learning. Now, each of the systems you studied in ground school takes on a new frame of reference as you begin your prestart checklist, testing and checking all the items you studied so hard. You'll learn flows, organized methods for preflighting the cockpit. There's one for each phase of flight: preflight, or "receiving;" before start; after start; taxi; before takeoff; climb; cruise; descent; approach; landing; after landing; parking; and termination. Learning the flow for each phase allows you to complete the necessary items first and then return with the checklist to double check each item.

Training intensifies.

As you move on to the sim portion of training, scheduling will become more and more critical. You're expected to be well prepared for each session, studying the upcoming maneuvers and doing a lot of "armchair" flying. To make your "cockpit" more realistic, you can tape the diagram of the panel layout onto the wall above your desk and make your simulated flight session more realistic.

You'll be busier than you ever expected. There will not be enough time in a day to sleep, eat, study, and attend your scheduled training sessions. Your assignments may range from early one morning (show up at 0500) to late the next evening (fly the 2000 to 0200 slot). There may be little or no consideration for how your body is taking all these odd hours. You will have to arrange your life carefully to make sure you're getting enough sleep and have adequate nourishment to think clearly during training sessions.

What happens next

Once you've completed training (sorry, there are no ceremonies for graduation or pinning of wings—just hurry up and wait), you'll be given some Initial Operating Experience (IOE), probably some 15 to 25 hours of flying with an experienced captain. Then will come the shock of getting tossed into the reserve pool, where you'll be back to waiting some more—first for the phone to ring and then, when it does, hurrying to get to the airport for a flight that should have left 20 minutes ago.

Your days off may be your own, but keep your plans tentative because often a three-day trip turns into a four-day event, thus spilling over to the Tuesday when you had planned to go somewhere or do something. Now your plans have to be canceled.

Depending on how fast your airline is growing or other pilots are leaving, you'll be on reserve, or on call, for two months to a year or more. You can request certain days off, but don't be surprised when they change your schedule or reroute your flight—and there go your plans for some R & R.

> The bottom line is flexibility. Learn to take changes in stride.

The bottom line is flexibility. Learn to take changes in stride. Remember that most of our business is sitting around waiting for something to happen—the phone to ring, the aircraft to arrive, the VOR checkpoint to pass, or seniority to improve in order to move up to a regular flying schedule for each month.

We've all done our share of waiting. My best advice is to fill your empty hours with something productive and beneficial. I've found it a great opportunity to learn a new skill or brush up on a rusty one, start a sideline business, or study for my next proficiency check. Whatever your choice, enjoy your "free time"—you'll never have enough of it!

Airline Culture: Do You Fit In?

"My airline never allows us to sleep in the crew room overnight; they lock the doors at 10 p.m." "Hey, if I need a room, I just call the coordinator and if there's a spare one, they'll give it to me." Confused by the contradictory rules and wonder what's going on? The preceding comments come from pilots at two major airlines, discussing their experience with the homeless crewmember dilemma. The regulations are actually two ends of a spectrum that will likely play a part in your flying future.

Each airline has its own unique flavor and way of doing things; learning how things are done at your "store" can be just as important as having the right technical skills to do the job. Some management types say that avoiding culture shock is the key to a long and happy career. Or said another way, getting your desired airline job is only one facet of your career; learning the tricks of the trade in order to keep that job will form another important part of your successful long-term survival.

Variations in style

Pilots in the aviation industry must learn the ins and outs of their particular flying world—whether it's a flight school with rules and regulations for students, a charter firm with client-pilot protocols, or a major airline that has a culture all its own. It's rare that you'll get a chance to sample a new environment before you are tossed into it and expected to swim easily after your first dunking. But thriving, rather than just surviving, in your new culture is extremely important to your success as an airline pilot.

Military pilots often have a better idea of what they'll encounter at an airline because they come from a background in which precision and structure are standard fare. They're used to doing things a certain way and following distinct protocols (both written and unwritten) that govern their daily workplace. On the other hand, GA pilots, when they've reached their long-sought goal, are quite surprised to learn about unwritten in-house rules of conduct.

Company styles can differ markedly. And we're not just talking about the obvious things like cargo versus passenger and domestic versus international, scheduled or charter. At many airlines there's a military style of life, punctuated by a strict hierarchy of who does what and when. Protocol governs almost everything from whose name goes in which slot on the hotel sign-in sheet to who gets first choice of crew meals to who gets the best seat on a deadhead flight. Other companies have a more casual style, with a less rigid, easygoing, let's-have-fun atmosphere where no one cares about such petty concerns. It's merely a matter of getting the job done right, period.

Just knowing how to fly isn't enough to succeed.

A number of factors will contribute to your success at a new job. New pilots who come to us for advice frequently want it all *now*. I can fly the airplane, no sweat, just feed me the ground school information and I'm ready for my airline pilot job. However, having a long, happy career aloft requires a lot more than just knowing how to fly. You would be very unhappy to land the job of your dreams and find that you were unable to hack the other 75 percent of the job. You must learn what nontechnical abilities you'll need to survive at an airline.

Your first year will normally be a probationary period, during which you'll be evaluated by other pilots you fly with, as well as by management and ground personnel. Your ability to fit in, do the job, and enjoy your interactions with others will be closely evaluated. Can you handle an irate flight attendant who figures you personally caused her to miss her flight home? Can you meet and greet customers according to company-defined guidelines? Do you enjoy the nonflying part of your job and display the helpful attitude you demonstrated during your job interview? Are you willing to learn and help others learn?

> Having a long, happy career aloft requires a lot more than just knowing how to fly. You must learn what nontechnical abilities you'll need to survive at an airline.

How about unexpected call-outs, cancelled days off, and rock bottom beginning wages? All of these can contribute to disillusionment with your once-hallowed "ideal career." One pilot we know began a job with a major airline following a stint as chief pilot at a regional airline. Thinking his former management position would yield some clout at his new job, he pulled various shenanigans, including telling crew schedulers how they could schedule him, implying that his former title had some value in his new position. As you can imagine, he soon alienated himself from management and line pilots alike.

Others have failed to recognize just what the job entails. Being available and ready to fly when you're on call is the name of the airline pilot game. Employee attendance, one of those areas they scrutinized closely during your interview, is very important; you're expected to live up to the good record you documented on your application. Calling in sick for illegitimate reasons—in retribution for a lousy flying schedule, for instance—will quickly find you a spot in front of the chief pilot doing the proverbial "rug dance."

A good attitude will pay off.

As your probationary year comes to a close, many airlines will require you to take a checkride in the simulator. If you've maintained a good-attendance and attitude record but your sim ride is less than stellar, a kindly check airman, who realizes you've got what it takes, may overlook your checkride jitters. On the other hand, if you've displayed an attitude that's less than enthusiastic, you could pass your probationary checkride but find yourself on the street for other unstated reasons during your 11th month of employment.

Attitude does affect your altitude (read profile) at an airline and is, perhaps, the number one criteria working in your favor. You are accountable for your actions and are expected to act like a responsible adult. Complaining that the company never recognizes or thanks you or gives you pats on the back is based on the childish expectation that all good deeds should be immediately rewarded. It's rather tough to give credit on an individual basis when you're one of perhaps thousands of pilots, flying hundreds of airplanes throughout the world, day in and year out.

Your reward can come from the personal satisfaction gained by going the extra mile, giving more than you take, volunteering for committees and projects to enhance and improve your work environment. Such behavior will be recognized when more tangible rewards become available. One day, when you need extra time off, your request to the Chief Pilot may be answered with a nod and a smile, because he's aware that you deserve the time in return for your ongoing good performance.

Adapting to a new environment

Patience, particularly at a large airline, is one key to success. If you see something that needs changing, work toward making it right but don't expect immediate results. Study the situation, gather the necessary data or suggestions, and present them in a logical, orderly manner. I did that early in my career when I found a much better alternative to our ground school's instructional radar video. I proposed the new vendor, sent a sample tape to the department head in charge of the curriculum, and grinned from ear to ear when my suggested replacement showed up on the classroom video monitor at the next year's class. Positive feedback from my coworkers proved that we had not only lowered the "nod-off" potential for after-lunch instruction but also provided valuable new weather information.

If you come to a major airline job with substantial experience at several other carriers, it's extremely important to shed your "but we did it this way at my old carrier" attitude. You have new challenges and opportunities; referring to the past can readily label you as a failed transplant who should hit the street if he can't adapt to the new agenda. This is not to say you can't integrate what you've learned from one carrier to the next—but do it seamlessly and using the right avenues.

Queries about how a certain procedure came into practice might net you the information you need to accomplish the transition smoothly or suggest a replacement at an appropriate time. All companies have policies or procedures you'll disagree with. Your job is to learn their system and, if you feel it necessary, provide a critique at an appropriate time. Remember that interview question about the time you complied with a policy or procedure even though you disagreed with it? Now you know what the interviewer was referring to and why he probed your ability to adapt to changes.

You can improve your lot and that of your fellow pilots by being proactive rather than reactive. If you see a problem, think of a positive way to discuss the situation. If you share your concerns with others and are flexible in your own needs, you'll find learning your airline's culture to be a snap. Your job satisfaction will improve markedly as you adapt to their culture and style.

The Exceptional Copilot: Is that you?

I recently received a brochure in the mail advertising a seminar to learn the skills they didn't teach you in flight school. Entitled the "Exceptional Co-Pilot" the brochure described a multitude of talents required for the successful first officer, including prioritizing; problem solving; managing time, resources, and crises; delegating; decision making; and developing political and people skills.

It sounded so good, I just couldn't resist reading on: assertiveness and responsibility; stress management; asking for what you want; giving and getting clear instructions; taking the initiative; and using all of your resources. With a hook like that, how could I *not* want to sign up immediately? Now, before you get too excited about this cure-all pilot course, let me tell you that it was actually entitled the "Exceptional Assistant" and was designed for teaching nonmanagement personnel how to achieve "respect as an indispensable secretary, administrative assistant, or support-staff member."

What immediately struck me was the similarity between those qualities listed as essential to succeed in almost any phase of the business world and those so crucial in the cockpit. Too often, we don't place sufficient emphasis on the importance of the non-flying skills needed to keep us alive and well in the microcosm of the flight deck. Whether there are one, two, or three pilots in your cockpit, these abilities are crucial to your success as a safe and competent airman. Let's take a look at each one and relate its importance to your role as a cockpit crewmember.

Prioritizing

Prioritizing is a key to managing the cockpit safely. Doing what's important NOW and leaving the secondaries until later can save your life. This is why there are checklists, so you don't have to make some of the standard decisions—both routine and emergency—over and over again.

However, many items don't have a clear-cut order, and it's up to you to decide their importance and timeliness. For example, getting the current weather is an all-important task that should be on your mind whenever you approach an airport. You need this information first (as early as possible, depending on radio reception distance) because it will help you with all the chores that follow, such as briefing the correct approach, making sense of the controller's instructions, and figuring your taxi route once you've landed and need to know which way to turn to get to the terminal or designated parking area.

Problem solving

Problem solving, the second seminar skill, is one reason we all enjoy aviation. Our job has constant challenges, involving the never-ending process of dealing with each mini-crisis as it arises. From descent planning to speed changes to finding and avoiding traffic conflicts, we spend the majority of our time aloft honing our problem-solving skills. Anyone wishing to succeed as a pilot should find these tasks challenging and fulfilling. The best pilots can handle multiple problems, prioritize them, solve them, and then move on to the next phase of flight, ready for another wave of decision making.

Managing time, resources, and crises

Managing time, resources, and crises is probably a good overall description of flying itself. Learning to widen your field of vision is called situational awareness—a key element in CRM and flight safety.

As aircraft become more sophisticated, we need to sharpen our management skills because the physical act of flying tends to fade into the background and becomes subordinate to the concept of working together. Many airlines will want you to have multipilot flight experience before they hire you, as proof that you can interact with others—in essence, that you *can* manage time and resources and deal with crises in an orderly, logical manner.

Delegating

Delegating is another skill learned in multipilot situations, although you can certainly start to work on it as a single pilot. Don't try to do everything yourself: use the resources around you. Many ex-military pilots who come from single-seat fighters find it hard to include others in their flying routine and stumble when it comes to developing an integrated cockpit-management crew.

Start your team building efforts early in your training by assigning traffic-watch duties to passengers, letting your students or instructor know what jobs you want their assistance with, and keeping ATC advised of any irregularities that could influence the safety of your flight. Clearly stating everyone's assigned duties will go a long way toward helping them manage priorities and achieve their goals.

Decision making

Decision making is learned through practice and observation. Probably the worst fears of all new captains revolve around making the wrong decisions. If we wanted to eliminate completely the possibility of making a wrong decision, we'd have to live in a vacuum. But you can improve your own decision-making skills by challenging yourself to a game of "What If?" Designed to make you think, it allows you to consider a situation, solicit input from various sources, and try out your own solutions without fear of making a fatal mistake.

Further expand your abilities by asking questions of those you fly with to determine their thinking processes in dealing with a particular situation. As you gain experience, you'll find the same logical thought processes being repeated over and over—your clue as to how to handle many of the situations you'll likely encounter when you're the one calling the shots.

> Probably the worst fears of all new captains revolve around making the wrong decisions. If we wanted to eliminate completely the possibility of making a wrong decision, we'd have to live in a vacuum.

Political and people skills

You can probably fill in the blanks when it comes to political and people skills. You know they're needed to survive in any interpersonal environment, and the cockpit is no different from the office or, for that matter, your own living room. Think about how you deal with difficult people and, if you're not comfortable with your solutions, resolve to work on those skills that are so important in promoting cockpit communication and harmony.

The Exceptional Copilot Has Many Skills

Good first officers, hard to come by, are greatly appreciated by captains everywhere. The exceptional copilot we decribed in the preceding article had many coveted skills. He was able to prioritize, problem solve, and manage time, resources, and crises. In addition, he could easily delegate and make decisions and he possessed good political and people skills. Quite a talent!

Now, let's consider some of the other skills that characterize the truly exceptional copilot: He is assertive and responsive; manages stress; asks for what he needs; provides what the captain needs and wants before being asked for it; gives clear instructions; and takes the initiative.

If you've done any reading on CRM, you'll realize that the days of the mild and meek first officer are long gone. Speaking up and making sure you assert your views is important, whether you fly solo or as part of a multipilot crew. As I emphasize during my initial crew briefing before each airline trip, "If you see anything you don't like, don't understand, or think is strange or weird, speak up! It takes two of us to fly this ship—and I value your input and experience."

Being assertive and responsible

The first officer's main job is to double as a watchdog and diplomat. Being assertive is a skill, the importance of which can't be overemphasized. Too many tales have been told of disastrous consequences resulting from someone not being willing or able to speak up. If you see something that isn't right, it's your duty to bring it to the captain's attention.

Assertiveness goes hand-in-hand with being responsible. Use your assertiveness in a responsible manner. If you see something that needs attention, mention it now for a quick resolution. Allowing situations to develop that could have easily been handled earlier is irresponsible and often dangerous. Use your diplomatic skills to advise the captain of important, safety-of-flight information in a timely manner.

> **Use your assertiveness in a responsible manner. If you see something that needs attention, mention it now for a quick resolution.**

Many times, using your assertiveness can easily relieve some of the stress associated with multipilot operations. It may take the form of questioning the other pilot(s) in an I-want-to-learn manner or discussing frankly your concerns about the operation in question. Identify and acknowledge a situation. It may be as simple as telling your coworker that you're pedaling as fast as you can and need a few more minutes to catch up or could use help with some of the tasks you've been assigned. Remember, recognizing your own limitations is an important part of CRM.

Managing cockpit stress

Cockpit stress can be relieved by consciously slowing your actions. Reminding yourself that you have to prioritize your duties and handle them one at a time will greatly reduce the stress that too often afflicts the new or overloaded first officer. Make a concerted effort to complete as many as possible of your duties ahead of time. The results will make you look good—well prepared and efficient—and put the captain at ease with your ability to do the job.

Asking for what you need

Asking for what you want is closely associated with being assertive. If you don't clearly state your needs, you've no one to blame but yourself. Whether you are making a request to ATC regarding a specific runway for landing or having the ground crew comply with an operational request, it's always important to make yourself heard—and understood—the first time.

Try to consider beforehand how an instruction will be received by the other person. Take just a moment before making your request to rerun the tape in your head and see if what you're about to say will be received as you intended. If not, rephrase it with a few simple explanations that make the request a logical one that's easy to understand. For example, you may have to preface a runway request to ATC with a short, concise explanation such as "Tower, our max tailwind limitation requires we use Runway 13, unable Runway 31." Or as I once said to Newark Tower, "Due to our malfunctioning gear doors, after landing we'll be unable to taxi clear of the runway until a mechanic inspects the gear and pins the doors in the up position." They undersood our operational needs after receiving my description, and that helped them focus on the problem, prompting a "cleared as requested" response. A bit of time expended in advance can go a long way toward helping others comprehend your exact situation.

Taking the initiative

Our last category, taking the initiative, is perhaps the hallmark of a good first officer. Having a thorough knowledge of the aircraft and its operational requirements can provide the necessary groundwork to initiate needed actions before they are required.

Because flying is nothing more than a well-orchestrated symphony of minievents, it's always a pleasure to work with someone who has planned ahead and is proactive, rather than reactive, in doing the job. Getting the ATIS before it's needed, completing the walk-around inspection early and noting any discrepancies or operational requirements, being familiar with the flight plan and weather for the trip, as well as staying ahead of the airplane and anticipating upcoming needs will benefit everyone, making the flight a safe and enjoyable one.

We've touched on some vital CRM skills that deserve much greater in-depth study. But in a nutshell, use your assertiveness responsibly, ask for what you want in a clear and concise manner, and take the initiative to become an exceptional copilot. Your job satisfaction will increase markedly as will the ease with which you'll be able to transition to that coveted Left Seat.

Glossary

A & P	Airframe and Powerplant
AIM	Airman's Information Manual
AOPA	Aircraft Owners and Pilots Association
ATC	Air Traffic Control
ATIS	Automatic Terminal Information Service (continuous prerecorded airport weather conditions)
ATP	Airline Transport Pilot
BFR	Biennial Flight Review
CFI	Certificated Flight Instructor
CFII	Certificated Flight Instructor Instruments
COM	Communication (vs. Navigation) radio
CRM	Crew (or Cockpit) Resource Management
CRQ	3-letter identifier for Carlsbad, California
DH	Decision Height (minimum altitude on an instrument approach)
DME	Distance Measuring Equipment
ETA	Estimated Time of Arrival
FAA	Federal Aviation Administration
FAR	Federal Aviation Regulation
FBO	Fixed Base Operator
FO	First Officer
FSS	Flight Service Station

GA	General Aviation
Hobbs Meter	Cockpit gauge recording accumulated airplane usage, normally based on engine oil pressure. Records in hours and tenths.
HSI	Horizontal Situation Indicator (compass instrument with superimposed navigation information)
IFR	Instrument Flight Rules
ICT	3-letter identifier for Wichita, Kansas
MAA	Maximum Authorized Altitude
MB	Millibars
ME	Multiengine
METAR	Meteorological Airman Report
MEI	Multi Engine Instructor
Navcom	Navigation and Communication radio
NDB	Non-Directional Beacon
NOS	National Ocean Survey (recently relabeled FAA charts)
NTSB	National Transportation Safety Board
Part 91	Section of FARs pertaining to non-commercial flying
PIC	Pilot in Command
RON	Remain overnight
RMI	Radio Magnetic Indicator
SES	Single Engine Sea
SIC	Second in Command
TAF	Terminal Area Forecast
TRW	Thunderstorm (with) Rain Shower
UAL	United Air LInes
VFR	Visual Flight Rules
VOR	Very (High Frequency) Omni (Directional) Radio (Range)
VOT	VHF Omni-directional Test signal